Planning Classroom Management

for Change

Karen A. Bosch

SkyLight
Professional
Development

Arlington Heights, Illinois

Planning Classroom Management for Change

Published by SkyLight Professional Development
2626 S. Clearbrook Drive, Arlington Heights, IL 60005-5310
Phone 800-348-4474, 847-290-6600
Fax 847-290-6609
info@skylightedu.com
http://www.skylightedu.com

Senior Vice President, Product Development: Robin Fogarty
Director, Product Development: Ela Aktay
Acquisitions Editor: Jean Ward
Senior Editor: Amy Kinsman
Editor: Judy Plazyk
Cover Designer: David Stockman
Book Designer: Bruce Leckie
Proofreader: Cathy Shapiro
Indexer: Candice Cummins Sunseri
Production Supervisor: Bob Crump
Production Assistant: Christina Georgi

ISBN 1-57517-157-0
LCCCN: 99-71040

2421-V
Item number 1727

Z Y X W V U T S R Q P O N M L K J I H G F E D C B
06 05 04 03 02 01 00   15 14 13 12 11 10 9 8 7 6 5 4 3 2

Acknowledgments

A very special acknowledgment goes to my husband, Gordon, daughter, Morghan, and son, Ryan, and his wife, Michele. Their support of my writing projects allows me to remain in front of the computer many days from dawn to late into the evening hours.

I am extremely grateful to my colleagues, Dr. Victor Culver and Annabel Sacks, for their editorial and research assistance. A special appreciation goes to Brittany Voyles for her enthusiasm and commitment to this project. I also want to thank the many preservice and practicing teachers who field-tested the classroom management process and the Observation Guide, wrote classroom management lesson plans, and shared their own classroom management plans in this book. Special recognition goes to the following people for their much appreciated efforts: Heide McCleery, Les Allen Fortune, Lindsay Crump Porzio, D.L. Achterfeld, Shreve Cassarino, Susan G. Smith, Brittany Voyles, Rebecca Barrett, Debra-Ann F. Brooks, Melanie A. Burnor, Sonya L. Huss, John C. Sammons, Linda M. Sherbinsky, Elizabeth T. Gardner, Holly L. Smith, Kimberly V. Ritter, and "K" Stone.

I am most appreciative to Judy Plazyk, editor of this text, for the professional guidance in preparing this text for publication. A special thanks goes to Jean Ward and Amy Kinsman at SkyLight Professional Development for being encouraging, yet patient, with the author's quest for perfection.

Contents

Preface

Over the past four years, I have initiated many discussions with teachers and asked them to describe classroom management. Although the term is widely used in education, the teachers I spoke with found the concept of classroom management difficult to verbalize, much less define. The following are some of their responses:

"I guess it is that difference in some classrooms."

"It is a hope, dream, a wish."

"All teachers want it. It is something that some teachers have and others do not. It is something I wish I had."

"It is magic!"

"It is what you need to be successful."

"If you are having trouble, you better get management."

"It is like law and order!"

"I read about it but I still don't know if I have it."

"You are lucky if you have it!"

Many books and articles are available to help teachers create a well-managed classroom. However, *Planning Classroom Management for Change* is unlike others because it offers the reader more than a definition of the term and a presentation of theorists and their ideas on classroom management. *Planning Classroom Management for Change* provides a model for classroom management by demonstrating it as a process. By following the steps in the process, teachers learn to observe and identify how classroom management works then develop and implement a personal classroom management plan (CMP) in their classrooms.

The contents of this book have been field-tested for more than four years. More than 100 preservice teachers in undergraduate and graduate education at Old Dominion University and undergraduate education at Virginia Wesleyan College, Norfolk, Virginia, used the CMP Observation Guide during their field experiences and wrote their own CMPs. In addition, twenty students from an alternative certification program at Old Dominion University, specifically, the Military Career Transition Program, have developed personal CMPs from this outline. Preservice teachers agreed that the classroom management Observation Guide kept them focused and on-task when they conducted classroom observations. One alternative program student said, "The Observation Guide served as an integrative activity that put all the content I was learning into a format that I could take directly to the classroom."

The Observation Guide has been reviewed by more than 100 practicing teachers for suggestions, clarifications, and feedback. In addition, fifteen Teachers of the Year from Virginia Beach and Chesapeake, Virginia, area schools participated in a summer program to review the guide and complete a CMP for possible use in this book. Ten school administrators and principals reviewed the manuscript, provided their perspective on classroom management, and described their expectations for how teachers and classrooms *should* work. One school administrator commented that this text finally makes classroom management approachable and available for all teachers. A principal stated that he is thrilled that someone has attempted to demystify this term and give all educators a chance to really know what classroom management is and how to pursue it. Discussion with the school administrators revealed that adopting and mandating a district-wide or even school-wide discipline approach has never worked because it soon became random, inconsistent, and arbitrary at the classroom level. They concluded that this book and its approach integrate concepts of teacher personality, management, and instruction as well as current thoughts on discipline and articulate them into a plan that can be successful in every classroom.

Several school personnel recruiters in Virginia thought it impressive that preservice teachers' portfolios included a personal classroom management plan. Upon hiring one of the graduates who participated in the CMP field-test, one superintendent of schools in Tennessee said that based on the CMP, he felt he was hiring an *experienced* teacher.

The time has come to replace, if not eliminate, the words *guess, hope, dream, wish, magic,* and *luck* from teachers' discussion of classroom management. The time has come to take the term *classroom management* and make it a process that can be taught, learned, and implemented in today's classrooms and the classrooms of the 21st century.

SkyLight Professional Development

Introduction

Fourth-grade teacher Steve Ames is about to conduct a science lesson on earthquakes. Having just placed their chairs in a semicircle in the center of the room, his students are not yet settled as they chat with their neighbors, their reading books closed in their laps. Steve places his chair in the center of the students and as he sits, he raises one finger. In seconds the students are silent, turning in their seats to face him. Steve raises a second finger, and the students open their books to the assigned pages. He asks the students to describe an earthquake. Several students raise their hands and Steve calls on each, listening intently and nodding approvingly as they each give their definition of an earthquake. When one student responds to another of Steve's questions without raising his hand, another student quietly reminds the outspoken student to wait his turn.

Is this scene merely a teacher's dream? No. It's a description of a typical lesson in Steve Ames' classroom. How does he do it? Steve Ames has a classroom management plan.

His classes were not always so organized. It once took too much time to get students to come to order, to pay attention. Too often, they were distracted by the antics of their fellow students or they wrote each other notes instead of doing their class work. When they did pay attention, they were reluctant to contribute to class discussions. But now the students are attentive and engaged in the lesson; often they work in teams to teach each other the lesson. They don't have time to get into trouble. They've accepted responsibility for the classroom environment, and they're not about to break the rules Steve asked them to create.

Overview of Classroom Management

Nearly every teacher agrees that classroom management is an important aspect of successful teaching. Fewer agree on how to achieve it, and even fewer claim that the concept of classroom management is operating in their own classrooms.

At one time the term *classroom management* was synonymous with discipline. Ten years ago, teachers asked to define classroom management in one word gave the following responses, in order of frequency: discipline, control, order, rules, and consequences. *Discipline* was always the first word they chose. In the last few years, however, teachers have responded with the following words in this order: control, organization, operation, consistency, student involvement, and discipline. In effect, discipline has become a much smaller part of the term classroom management. Classroom management is much more than any one of these words or the sum of all these words.

Classroom management means how the teacher works, how the class works, how the teacher and students work together, and how teaching and learning happens. For students, classroom management means having some control in how the class operates and understanding clearly the way the teacher and students are to interact with each other. For both teachers and students, classroom management is not a condition but a process!

Classroom Management: Gift or Skill?

Many teachers, especially beginning teachers, cite classroom management as an ever-present concern (Veenman 1984). A meta-analysis of the past 50 years of classroom research identified classroom management as the most important factor, even above student aptitude, having an effect on student learning (Wang, Haertel, and Walberg 1994). But contrary to popular belief, classroom management is not a gift bestowed upon some teachers.

While it's true that some teachers adapt to classroom management techniques easily, making it look to their colleagues like they possess some innate talent, classroom management is a skill, a skill that can be taught like any other, and, most importantly, a skill that like any other must be practiced to achieve proficiency.

Although much has been written about classroom management, teachers have not received comprehensive, practical methods of improving classroom management, and little emphasis has been placed on "helping teachers understand the issues in effective classroom management and the relationship among various strategies . . . " (Jones and Jones 1995, 1).

Many teachers try classroom management ideas and strategies, tossing them spontaneously and inconsistently into the classroom, then become discouraged when the classroom they hope for does not materialize. Effective classroom management does require specific skills such as planning, organizing, and reflecting as well as an aptitude for teamwork and perseverance. It requires a great deal of commitment initially then a willingness to adjust one's thinking and actions as one learns what works and what doesn't.

But teachers cannot implement a definition. When teachers see that classroom management is a process, a process they can follow, learn, and implement in their own classrooms, they understand that they can tailor the process to match their specific skills and needs. In other words, they can set themselves up for success, not failure. In addition, they recognize that the process is ongoing. Just as teachers change with experience and the changing needs of their students, so their classroom management plan must adapt as well.

Creating a Classroom Management Plan

A classroom management plan (CMP) is not only a means of organizing a classroom. The plan gives structure to everything that goes on in the classroom—from the seating arrangement to the lessons to the grading of homework assignments to the relationships among classmates. As an antenna eliminates static, improving television reception, so a CMP eliminates distractions and allows teachers to focus on teaching and students to focus on learning. And because teachers and students alike know exactly what to expect in the classroom, the plan fosters a sense of community, of everyone working toward the same goal.

There is no magic formula for creating a CMP. In fact, while all teachers may have similar components in their CMPs, no two plans will be the same. That's because to be effective, a CMP must reflect a teacher's personality and teaching style. It will work precisely because the teacher feels comfortable with it. The purpose of *Planning Classroom Management for Change* is to guide teachers in the preparation of a CMP. The text takes teachers through the process of creating a personal CMP, a process that has proved effective with numerous teachers.

The Classroom Management Process

The process of creating a CMP consists of five steps. In the first step, teachers must reflect on their own teaching practices and experiences and in written form describe not only their teaching goals but their strengths and weaknesses both as teachers and as human beings. Second, teachers must scrutinize their classroom and their teaching practices objectively in the same way they would observe a colleague's classroom. Observing another classroom is also recommended. The third step is initial development of the classroom management plan using what one has learned in the reflection and observation steps. The fourth step is implementation of the plan in the classroom. Teachers must teach their students the plan just as they would any subject. The fifth and final step is the refinement and revision of the plan based on student input and reflection on the success or failure of aspects of the current plan.

How to Use this Book

The first six chapters in *Planning Classroom Management for Change* describe the CMP and the five steps of the process of creating it. Questions, activities, and examples throughout the text help teachers further explore and understand classroom management as a process. Descriptions of how teachers can use a CMP appear in each chapter. Some of these examples are fictional; others are based on actual teacher accounts of the value of the CMP in their classrooms.

Chapter 1, Classroom Management, discusses the need for classroom management, describes the CMP, and outlines the five steps in the process of creating a CMP: reflection, observation, development, implementation, and reflection and revision.

Chapter 2, Reflection: Getting in Touch with Your Teaching Self, describes the first step in the process of creating a CMP. The classroom management process begins with introspection. The questions and activities in chapter 2 are designed to assist the teacher in identifying his or her teaching self. Teacher reflection also includes the thought processes teachers engage in outside the classroom. Getting in touch with their thoughts, attitudes, and personality styles, both inside and outside the classroom, allows teachers to focus the CMP to strengthen personal weak areas and capitalize on strong ones.

Having identified thought processes and other internal characteristics, the next step is for teachers to step outside themselves and observe their teaching practices and behaviors. The classroom management Observation Guide in Chapter 3, Observation, helps teachers observe and record specific classroom information, which they then use to develop their CMP. The See, Hear, and Feel Method helps teachers record the classroom setting and operation. Other sections help teachers collect information on classroom management in operation—what it is, how it works, when it works, and why it works. Teachers are also encouraged to visit other classrooms and interview other teachers.

In the third step of the classroom management process, described in Chapter 4, Developing a Personal CMP, the teacher composes his or her own CMP. The information gathered in chapters 2 and 3 serves as a resource in developing the personal CMP.

Chapter 5, Implementing the CMP, focuses on how to teach the CMP to the class, the implementation step of the process. In addition to guidance on planning and writing lessons to teach the CMP, this section offers step-by-step lessons teachers can incorporate into the curriculum.

A teacher's personal CMP remains a dynamic, ever-changing script for classroom management. Reflecting on the CMP during the implementation phase is important. Chapter 6, Reflecting on and Revising the CMP, focuses on this reflective thinking and offers a method that turns reflection into revision and thinking into action. Teachers can plan reflection time into a daily or weekly school schedule, allotting from as little as fifteen minutes to as much as thirty minutes of time.

Chapter 7, Samples of Effective Teachers' CMPs, offers four sample CMPs from teachers of primary, intermediate, middle, and secondary grades to give further guidance on creating an effective CMP.

Applications of the Classroom Management Process

Planning Classroom Management for Change meets an important need for both preservice and practicing teachers. The term *preservice teacher* refers to a student enrolled in a teacher education program and involved with field experiences from the initial levels of classroom observation to the student teaching experience. A *practicing teacher* currently teaches in a classroom.) The classroom management process is easy to teach, learn, and implement. It can be done by everyone involved with classroom teaching. It can be done individually, by teams, by grade levels, or as a school-wide effort. It can be taught to any number of teachers at one time or any combination of teachers. For example, it could be an inservice activity for a school, all sixth-grade teachers, all math teachers, all first year teachers, all teachers needing remediation, and so on. For remediation purposes, principals and teachers must often devise a self-improvement plan. The process described in this book provides a direct, responsive, nonthreatening plan for improvement.

Planning Classroom Management for Change is aimed primarily at practicing and preservice teachers, although others involved in education will also find the information extremely useful. Undergraduate and graduate teacher education students could use it as a primary text in methods courses in education, observation, and field experience and in the student teaching experience. Teacher education programs can require preservice teachers to make observations throughout the program and require development of a personal CMP for use in the first year of teaching.

The CMP could be included in a teacher's portfolio, which is used in the interview stages of recruitment. In addition to the portfolio she presented during interviews with school system recruiters, one preservice teacher compiled a mini portfolio to leave with school principals after an interview. This mini portfolio included a resume, a teaching philosophy statement, a CMP, specific lesson and unit plans, letters of recommendation, and evaluations from field experiences. The feedback she received indicates that the CMP, portfolio, and mini portfolio are valuable assets in securing a teaching position.

The description of the classroom management process is particularly helpful to the alternative certification student. The alternative certification program, usually a shorter, condensed preparation, requires fewer field-based experiences. This text highlights the most important information in organizing a classroom and structuring teacher and student autonomy. An alternative certification student writes, "My CMP has become my learning rubric. I am beginning to understand how we learn, what can impede us in the learning process, what strategies will work for me, and how to structure those strategies into a CMP."

Facing their first teaching job, many new teachers worry about what to do first. Beginning, maintaining, and ending the year with a management plan can alleviate some of this apprehension. In addition, this book provides an opportunity for both preservice and practicing teachers to prepare before the first year of teaching or the school year begins.

Many practicing teachers who may feel burned out or ready to give up or who want more from teaching would benefit from constructing or reconstructing a plan for classroom management. Teachers returning to the profession can prepare a CMP before entering the classroom. Teachers changing grade levels can construct a CMP appropriate to that grade level before the year begins. Teachers moving from school to school, area to area, state to state can take the CMP with them.

Principals, school administrators, district supervisors, and superintendents can endorse this classroom management process because it offers consistency, efficiency, and effectiveness in setting standards of classroom operation. It is easy to implement as a school-wide and district-wide policy. Knowing what to do and how to do it, faculty and staff can assist and support each other. A team of teachers can develop a CMP together by grade level or subject area.

This book can support teacher induction programs. The classroom management process developed in this book gets to the heart of the concerns and problems of teachers searching for classroom management. The book can help both mentor and mentee establish a cooperative dialogue in communicating essentials of teaching, collecting and sharing information, developing a CMP, and reflecting on specific information for professional growth and development.

The Importance of a Classroom Management Plan

Public education is important to nearly all Americans, and the public's concerns are high on the national agenda. According to the 30th Annual Phi Delta Kappa/Gallup Poll of the Public's Attitudes toward the Public Schools, 18 percent of respondents awarded the nation's public schools a grade of A or B, and 46 percent of respondents rated their local public schools a grade of A or B. This year, the two reported greatest concerns people had about public schools were concern about fighting/violence/gangs (15%) and lack of discipline/more control (14%). The public has established a priority that discipline and order return to schools (Rose and Gallup 1998). In *Education 97/98*, Elam, Rose, and Gallup state the following:

> One of the principal goals of education is to produce individuals capable
> of clear moral judgment and self-control. But in the real school world,
> establishing a climate for the development of self-control as well as for

academic achievement often requires the exercise of external authority and control (33).

Educators know that, ultimately, exercising external authority and control is not the answer. The answer lies within people. Self-control is an educational goal that needs to be developed in schools. *Planning Classroom Management for Change* contains a format that assists a beginning or practicing teacher, a teacher new to a school system, a teacher new to a grade level, and even a teacher seeking remediation. The hope is the text challenges school administrators, teachers, and teacher educators to rethink the rhetoric of classroom management. It adds promise to teacher preparation programs and teachers seeking to improve their teaching by making classroom management a process and, therefore, accessible to every teacher and every classroom. *Planning Classroom Management for Change* can place teachers and students in a position to meet the demands for higher standards, more discipline in the classrooms, and improved student learning.

Chapter 1

Classroom Management

First-year teacher Kathryn Flaherty was ecstatic when she was offered the position teaching third grade at Meadowlark Elementary School. She spent the weeks before school started decorating her classroom with colorful posters and artwork, rearranging the desks into perfect rows, making sure she had plenty of supplies from whiteboard markers to blank transparencies for the overhead. A stickler for details, she had the first three weeks of lessons worked out and written neatly in her lesson planner. She knew the subjects she would cover forward and backward and felt she was prepared for any questions the students might have.

On the first day of class, she greeted her students enthusiastically and started right in on her first lesson. But her carefully made lesson plans did not tell her what to do when the students didn't pay attention day after day. They didn't help her cope with one particularly ill-behaved student whose antics, while not destructive or harmful, were a constant distraction to the other students. They didn't tell her how to get students to respond to her excellent open-ended questions. When she placed the students in pairs or groups of three to work, they, and she, accomplished even less. When a friend phoned her to inquire about her first weeks on the job, Kathryn said simply, "I was doing just fine until the kids showed up."

Clearly Kathryn didn't have a Classroom Management Plan (CMP). A teacher with a CMP will not look or feel like a beginner. With the support of the CMP, a teacher sends a message not only to students but to administrators and parents that she knows what she is doing.

What Is Classroom Management?

Les Fortune, a Virginia Beach, Virginia, Teacher of the Year, writes: "Classroom management is the most misunderstood term in the educator's vocabulary. All teachers seek it, parents expect it, and administrators demand it. Should an administrator enter the classroom for an observation, the teacher is most cognizant that his or her performance will be judged primarily on the merits of viewed classroom management—not learning, a far more difficult accomplishment to measure."

The quote above underscores the conundrum that is classroom management—it's tough to define but everyone knows when it's not there. This teacher effectively characterizes both the significant and the intangible nature of classroom management. But classroom management need not be so elusive. The purpose of the classroom management plan (CMP) is to put, literally and figuratively, the tools for classroom management in teachers' hands.

In a nutshell, a CMP structures teaching and student learning and autonomy and provides a sense of community in a classroom. But the best way to describe and define a CMP is to discuss each of its components and their effect on classroom management. The four primary components of the CMP are classroom organization, instruction, student assessment, and teacher reflection.

The Components of a Classroom Management Plan

Classroom Organization

Classroom organization supports teacher instruction and student learning. It encompasses the classroom environment—the physical aspects such as lighting, temperature, decorations, and the set-up, comfort, and proximity of furniture—and the classroom operation—aspects the teacher imposes such as rules, routines, consequences, and incentives.

Classroom environment

The physical environment should make students enjoy coming to class. The room should be bright and welcoming, with student work displayed on the walls and bulletin boards. Most important, students should feel safe there.

The placement of desks must allow students to view the chalkboard and the screen used with the overhead projector and allow the teacher to access the desks easily. The classroom should have traffic patterns carefully established for frequent activities such as to reach the pencil sharpener, go to the board, and exit the room.

The environment makes it easier or more difficult to implement classroom management. For example, the seating arrangement can support or discourage the aim of a lesson. Straight rows with the teacher's desk in front may be neat and orderly, but this arrangement contributes little to a sense of classroom community. Desks arranged in a semi-circle or groups of four promote discussion and working and learning together. The teacher's desk in the back of the room instead of the front signals that the students are the most important part of the class. Students' work displayed on the bulletin boards, interactive bulletin boards for instruction and improved learning, and student-designed bulletin boards not only enhance the environment but give students a role in planning that environment.

Classroom operation

The other aspect of classroom organization is the formulated policies, rules, incentives, consequences, established routines, and procedures that fall under the heading of classroom operation. Perhaps the most important item under classroom operation is rules.

Whether the teacher refers to them as rules, rights, expectations, or responsibilities, these principles govern classroom operation and become the written and unwritten code that allows a classroom to work. The classroom is set up as a democracy, with teacher and students working together to create and enforce the rules and establish guidelines for behavior. The rules created by teacher and students support a task-oriented learning community in which teacher and students share expectations. Once they have a role in making the classroom work, students become more accountable for how it works. All students must understand the rules, and everyone must know the consequences for not following rules.

Consequences are a part of every classroom. Teachers should solicit student input in establishing consequences as well as rules. Students then choose their behavior with full understanding of the consequences, and, one hopes, they choose discipline and self-control. The use of rules and consequences students help create teaches them that they are accountable for their actions and as a result builds students' feelings of self-reliance and self-respect.

Routines and procedures are a vital part of efficient classroom operation. Routines help with everyday administrative tasks such as taking attendance and recording lunch options. Other examples of daily routines include the teacher greeting students at the door every morning, the pledge of allegiance, and the recitation of the class motto as well as journal writing, copying objectives from the chalkboard, responding to a verbal or math challenge, reading aloud to students after lunch, and a ten-minute pack down just before school ends. Procedures might cover the proper time and way to request use of the bathroom pass and pencil sharpener, to turn in homework and in-class assignments, or to seek teacher assistance.

Teachers send messages, spoken and unspoken, to students all day long. Students send such messages as well. These messages are commonly referred to as cues. Cues are the nonverbal and verbal signs, signals, gestures, and body language teachers and students use to communicate with each other without using the standard way of speaking. Teachers can use this form of communication to send specific messages and expectations quickly and efficiently. For example, to begin a lesson a teacher's cue might be raising his hand and moving to the center of the room. Another teacher might raise her index finger to her lips, a cue requesting silence. Students enjoy learning cues and assuming responsibility for responding to the cues appropriately without the teacher speaking a word.

Many teachers include incentives in their classroom operation. Teachers need to think carefully about incentives and decide the role they wish incentives to play in their classroom. If offered, incentives must be relevant, age appropriate, inviting, fun, desired, and readily chosen over the consequences. Incentives can create and sustain effort, persistence, enthusiasm, satisfaction, and empowerment.

The terms *incentives* and *rewards* are often used interchangeably in education literature; however, incentives are much more than rewards. Incentives are a way to help a student choose to work toward a goal, while reward suggests the behavior is not inherently worthwhile but requires a prize to accomplish. Using the term incentive implies acceptance of some responsibility and a focus on learning rather than a focus on the reward. Even more simply, rewards are thought of as receiving something, whereas incentives are accomplishing something. Incentives can help promote goals, reinforce learning, maintain effort, enhance achievement, create enthusiasm, alter attitudes, promote self-control, strengthen appropriate behaviors, and achieve desired behaviors. Most important, incentives are fun, user friendly, risk-free, and inexpensive motivators. Incentives provide teachers with a powerful alternative to discipline, reprimands, threats, yelling, and telling. Often incentives provide the classroom with a sense of community, comradery, and satisfaction as students work together to accomplish the goals of the incentives (see Figure 1.1).

FIGURE 1.1

Types of Incentives

Incentives can be defined as encouragers and reinforcers to accomplishing appropriate behaviors.

B. F. Skinner defines reinforcers as "reinforcing stimuli and . . . anything individuals experience or receive following a certain behavior that serves to strengthen that behavior" (Charles 1999, 32). He divides reinforcers into the following four categories (Charles 1999):

- Social reinforcers: words, gestures, facial expressions and behaviors that strengthen student behavior such as "Excellent," "Nice going," "I like that," or smiles, winks, thumbs up
- Graphic reinforcers: check marks, stars, stickers
- Activity reinforcers: activities students choose such as parties, games, free time, talk time, extra recess, free reading
- Tangible reinforcers such as popcorn, candy, pencils, pens, decals, certificates, and happy grams.

Incentives can be the catalyst for students to improve their behavior, increase their academic involvement, strive for progress, and earn success. Their effects can be seen, heard, and felt in classrooms. Teachers whose CMP has a well-designed incentive component can see students making choices to work toward accomplishing incentives. They can see students work together and hear students support each other in achieving incentives. The classroom is a place students feel more accountable and successful in achieving their learning goals and needs.

Instruction

The second component of the CMP is instruction. It has two parts: lessons and effective teaching practices. Classroom management and instruction work together to enhance the teaching and learning processes. As it underlies the procedures, responsibilities, expectations, body language, cues, and instructional, preventive, supportive, and corrective strategies, the CMP supports teaching and learning and allows learning to happen.

Lessons

A CMP can help teachers plan and write lessons as it offers a kind of checklist to make sure they have included all the most important elements of effective instruction. These elements include clear objectives, an engaging presentation, active student involvement, good questioning and response techniques, varied activities addressing various learning styles, monitoring student understanding, and individualized instructional strategies.

When teachers plan lessons, they determine the objectives of the lesson, decide how to introduce the topic, ascertain the most effective way to convey the information, and select activities that promote student understanding. The instructional strategies they choose capitalize on students' needs, interests, prior knowledge, and abilities.

The range of instructional and learning strategies teachers can use is broad and varied. Some instructional strategies are brainstorming, modeling and discussion, the use of graphic organizers, open-ended questions, guided practice activities, transparencies, and hand-outs. Student learning strategies include individual, pair, and larger-group activities. These and other instructional and learning strategies for both individual students and the entire class are discussed in greater depth in chapters 3 and 4.

In addition to strategies and techniques, teachers must have a way to monitor the success of a lesson. Monitoring refers to observing and collecting information about each student's understanding of the lesson. Students should also learn to monitor their own learning. The teacher must give students the opportunity to evaluate themselves, and the CMP outlines the ideas and strategies that promote self-evaluation.

Success-building strategies increase students' participation and effort in learning and behaving more appropriately. These strategies range from giving thorough reviews before tests to using portfolios for assessment purposes. An understanding of Howard Gardner's multiple intelligences helps teachers develop success-building strategies for alternative style learners (1993). These and other strategies are discussed in chapter 4.

Teachers must also have a plan for the use of classroom technology such as computers and video and audio equipment. Other resources available for classroom use include newspapers, transparencies, games, maps, globes, pictures, reference books, pamphlets, posters, manipulatives, and the human element—guest speakers. The process of creating the CMP requires teachers to think through the resources available and needed to teach the curriculum ahead of time and plan better use of these resources.

Effective teaching practices

Specific teacher behaviors and practices not only enhance instructional time and student learning, but they can reduce discipline problems, decrease interruptions, and minimize student off-task behaviors. The effectiveness of classroom management becomes apparent when it creates the atmosphere needed for students to learn and for the class to work together. Simply put, learners need a positive classroom atmosphere and a teacher who offers positive reinforcement and support. Other effective teaching behaviors include having a positive attitude, building positive relationships among classmates, fostering student social skills, developing preventive and supportive discipline strategies, promoting problem-solving and decision-making skills, and encouraging student self-control.

Classroom management can have its greatest impact in the prevention of classroom discipline problems. Classroom management is found in the strategies teachers choose to *prevent* classroom or student situations or problems from occurring or escalating and the strategies they use to elicit *support* from the class and individual students in situations of frustration, confrontation, and intervention.

Both preventive and supportive discipline strategies begin with developing a sense of community in the classroom. Teachers must work to get students to like each other, work and learn together, and be accountable for how the class works. They must also work to get students to like them and work for and learn from them. Establishing positive relationships and providing a student-centered, user-friendly, and risk-free environment becomes a class responsibility. The CMP can structure the ideas, strategies, and procedures for how the class operates and how the class and individual students respond. For example, a teacher can teach students a signal to use to express frustration so the teacher can go to the student immediately before the situation reaches a boiling point. The CMP can have procedures to reduce frustration such as allowing students to ask a buddy for help or allowing them a time-out so they can remove themselves from the situation for needed perspective. In times of confrontation, the class motto and policy can assist students in making good behavior choices and having a commitment to solving the problem. Because rules and consequences have been developed by the class, they are easier for students to follow and accept. Peer support, approval, and expectations help prevent and assist in solving many difficult and time-consuming classroom situations.

Students learn more and behave better in classrooms that meet their basic needs, and the need to belong is important to all members of the class. But often students' social skills are underdeveloped or they don't have a collective sense about working together for the common good. Strategies such as discussing and debating social issues, expressing personal opinions, reviewing current events, evaluating pros and cons of an issue, and employing conflict-resolution methods can help students develop social skills and see the classroom as a community.

Conflict-resolution methods are techniques the class develops for solving problems, preventing fighting, reducing tattling, and just getting along together. To solve problems, for example, teachers might give students procedures such as "Ask three before me," in which students ask three other students for their opinions and help to make a decision. A procedure to prevent fighting might include teaching students first, to back off; second, to leave the other student's space; and third, to count to ten. A procedure to prevent tattling might include listing this problem on the agenda for discussion at the next class meeting.

Linked with conflict-resolution strategies are problem-solving and decision-making strategies and self-management techniques that help students develop self-control. Any ideas, procedures, or tasks students can implement without teacher assistance give them a sense of independence, autonomy, and feelings of importance. Students need opportunities to learn how to behave in school, how to act in public and private, and how to be responsible people and citizens. A procedure such as the personal problem/solution plan (PPSP), which is a way to respond to confrontation with another person, teaches students self-control. The steps of the PPSP are first, to ignore the other person; next, to ask the person politely to stop; third, to ask the person to stop in a loud voice so others hear; and, finally, to ask a teacher or adult for help solving the problem (Bosch and Kersey 1993). Such strategies provide both teachers and students with methods to resolve conflicts. Additional strategies appear in Chapter 4.

Kohn (1996) suggests that teachers must work toward providing supportive environments in which students are included as collaborators in solving class problems. Regular class meetings give students an opportunity to take responsibility for the way the class works and the way each student works in the classroom. In class meetings, students make decisions, solve problems, and agree to make changes to improve classroom situations.

Assessment

While necessary, the third component of the CMP is one both students and teachers often find disagreeable. Student assessment conjures thoughts of subjectivity and unfairness. It remains an all too active, threatening, and coercive component in classrooms. With the help of the CMP and its clear outline of grading procedures, students not only understand the grading process, they feel they have some effect on their grades.

Teacher Reflection

Reflective teaching practices—the fourth component of the CMP—are planned opportunities to think about teaching in general, recall a specific lesson, or think about how to help an individual student. Some reflective practices are journal writing, meeting with colleagues, or simply quiet, focused thinking time. One aspect of reflective thinking practices is monitoring one's own teaching practices.

Teachers can monitor their teaching and classroom management to learn more about what they are really like as teachers, how they teach, manage, and interact with students, and how to achieve greater teacher effectiveness and learner success. Completing the self-evaluation activities in Chapter 2 and the observations in Chapter 3 helps teachers learn more about their teaching and how to teach.

The Classroom Management Process

Creating an effective CMP that incorporates all of these components—from classroom organization and instruction to student assessment and teacher reflection—is a five-step process. Teachers with a CMP have more than a "plan on paper": completing the process provides their classrooms with structure and creates a sense of community in a classroom. The five steps of the classroom management process are reflection, observation, development, implementation, and reflection and revision. Chapters 2 through 6 discuss each step in the process and offer guidance and activities to help teachers complete each step.

In brief, the first step, reflection, asks teachers to evaluate their teaching practices and experiences both positive and negative. The second observation step requires teachers to observe their classroom and teaching practices objectively in light of what they learned about themselves in the first step. The third step is initial development of the CMP. The fourth step is implementation of the plan in the classroom. The final step has teachers solicit student input to the plan as well as reflect on the plan's success in its current form. This last step is an ongoing process throughout a teacher's career.

It's important to note that teachers could simply fill out the CMP template (see Figure 4.1 in chapter 4) and believe they have a plan for classroom management. But it is the process that helps teachers improve their classroom management skills, not the answers to the CMP questions. For through the process, teachers internalize the responses. Through the process, teachers face their strengths and weaknesses as educators, learn to evaluate objectively their teaching effectiveness, and perhaps most importantly come to understand that as they grow and change, so must the CMP. The very act of completing the process makes a teacher a better teacher.

Chapter 2

Reflection: Getting In Touch with Your Teaching Self

Jennifer Hansen, the newest faculty member at Jacobs Middle School, entered the faculty lounge, placed the stack of papers she was carrying on the couch and plopped down beside the pile. Kate Weber looked up from her writing when her young friend let out a huge sigh.

"Whew!" Jennifer exclaimed. "Thank heavens this day is over."

"Rough one?" Kate asked.

"That's an understatement. It seems everything went wrong today. I even had one student fall asleep during my lecture on the Constitution."

"We all have days like that. We just have to make sure they don't happen too often. That's why I have this," she said and held up a spiral-bound notebook.

"What's that?" Jennifer asked, leaning forward to get a closer look.

"My teaching journal. I was just reflecting on a lesson I taught today that didn't go as well as I'd hoped."

"You're writing about it?!" Jennifer asked, incredulously. "I don't want to think about this day ever again. In fact, I just want to forget it ever happened. It's done. It's over. That's that."

"Then how will you fix it?"

"Fix it?"

"Ever hear the saying, 'Those who cannot remember the past are condemned to repeat it?'"

"Sure. George Santayana. But tomorrow's another day. I'll start fresh then."

"So you know what went wrong?"

"Oh, sure," Jennifer grinned. "The weather's getting warmer. My students were thinking about baseball and in-line skating. They weren't interested in the Bill of Rights."

"Well, the weather's going to keep getting warmer. Of course, you could wait until fall to get their attention again . . . or you could think now about ways to get them interested in the Bill of Rights."

Suddenly Jennifer stopped smiling. "You're serious, aren't you? How often do you write in that journal?"

"Every day," replied Kate.

"But you've been teaching, what, eight years! Don't you have all your lessons planned out? Don't you teach the same lessons each year?"

"Well, yes, each year I cover American History from the Pilgrims landing at Plymouth Rock to the Gulf War, so the topics are the same, but the lessons themselves aren't. Each class is different, students change every year—how can my lessons stay the same?" Kate queried.

"Wow, I had no idea. Looks like I'm the one getting a valuable lesson today. So tell me about this reflecting idea. What exactly do you do?"

"Every day I make notes to myself on two things that worked that day and two things that didn't. I also jot down something new I learned, whether it was something a student taught me or something they and I discovered together."

Jennifer lifted a finger to stop her friend, reached hurriedly for a pad of paper and a pen, then with pen poised to write, she nodded for Kate to continue.

"You can reflect on your teaching in whatever way is comfortable for you. Sometimes I make a Venn diagram at the end of a unit. I poll students about what they liked about the unit, then in one circle I list what they liked and in the other circle what I liked, and I see what matches. Sometimes instead of writing, I'll sit down with a colleague and we'll discuss our day, just like we're doing now. We can learn a lot from each other, you know."

"Do you mind if I tell you about my lesson today?" Jennifer asked. "Maybe you can give me some pointers."

Analyze Your Teaching Self

The classroom management process begins with introspection, which eventually leads to the sort of reflection Kate and Jennifer discuss in the scenario above. Jennifer has realized that she must take the time to reflect on the lesson that didn't go well, but to be a truly effective teacher, Jennifer also needs to reflect on her strengths as a person and convert those strengths to professional strengths, using them to improve her classroom and help her students get more out of their lessons.

Teachers need to analyze their personal and teaching selves because they need to be mindful of who they are and can be in a classroom. By learning more about themselves, teachers can enhance both their teaching and their classroom management skills. In this chapter, teachers complete a questionnaire to begin the classroom management process. The introspective nature of the questions helps teachers identify their attitudes, beliefs, goals, strengths, and weaknesses so they can incorporate them into their classroom management plans (CMPs). Once they recognize their personal strengths and weaknesses, they can use their strengths as assets to classroom management and recognize their weaknesses as areas needing support in their CMP. The reflection questionnaire gives teachers a starting point from which to develop their personal CMPs. Thus, they first observe within, then they move to the next step in the classroom management process and observe without, reflecting on their teaching selves in action in Chapter 3.

The purpose of this reflection is to ensure the CMP fits the teacher. The CMP can work only if the teacher feels comfortable with it. While one teacher's plan may share many components with the plan of a teacher down the hall or even all the other fourth-grade teachers, ultimately, the teacher must personalize the plan for it to be successful.

The questionnaire also helps bridge the gap between one's personal self and the teaching self. Many teachers think it best to keep their personal and professional lives separate, but truly effective teachers find ways to incorporate their personal style and interests into their classroom, and their answers on the reflection questionnaire can help them do that. A teacher who enjoys art or music can incorporate these subjects into lessons, making them more interesting for the teacher and, as a result, for students. Using different approaches also provides the variety that appeals to alternate style learners who may have trouble with the verbal/linguistic, mathematical/logical bent of traditional lessons. Auditory learners, for example, might respond particularly well to lessons that incorporate music. Teachers with a flair for the dramatic might let students perform skits or conduct interviews to demonstrate their understanding of a particular lesson. Identifying his or her particular skills and talents is a teacher's first step to using them to good effect in the classroom.

Reflection Questionnaire

The questions in the Reflection Questionnaire (see Figure 2.1) have no right or wrong answers. They are intended to get you thinking and promote further understanding of your teaching self—not just as you complete the questions but every day of your teaching life.

To stimulate your thinking about your own answers to these questions, read the discussion section that follows, which includes how other teachers have responded to the questions. Take the time to consider the discussion questions as well to help you delve deeper into the question and your answer.

Discussion of the Reflection Questionnaire

1. What does the term *classroom management* mean to you?

Heide, a practicing fourth-grade teacher for twenty-nine years, describes classroom management as "those skills needed by a teacher to establish and maintain a learning environment in which students are taught to be independent and accountable as they assume increasing responsibility for their own learning and conduct."

Shreve, a practicing teacher for one year, writes "Classroom management isn't how quiet your room is or how frightened your students are into behaving but rather how motivated and interdependent your students are in their work. Classroom management is teamwork."

Often, teachers define classroom management in terms of what they think others think it means. For example, if the principal stresses that classroom management simply means good discipline, the teacher must assume that

Reflection Questionnaire

1. What does the term *classroom management* mean to you?

2. Reflect on your philosophy of education. Write five "I believe" statements about teaching.

3. List your strengths. Think about both personal strengths and talents. Circle those that particularly apply to classroom teaching.

4. Ask several family members and friends to tell you what they like best about you, and list their responses below. Note responses similar to yours.

5. List your weaknesses. Circle those the CMP may need to support.

6. List the most important qualities you wish to foster in your students.

7. How do you introduce yourself to the class?

8. Complete a concept map on "What Is Good Teaching?"

9. Write a brief paragraph on how you make a difference in the lives of your students.

10. Find and copy a favorite quote, poem, or story that conveys an understanding of your teaching self.

FIGURE 2.1
SkyLight Professional Development

definition to fulfill the principal's expectations and, of course, receive a good evaluation. However, that meaning may limit the term's potential and, ultimately, a teacher's potential and effectiveness in a classroom.

The first step in understanding the term classroom management is to separate it from the literature and what others think it means, and find your own definition of this term. Ask yourself what this term means to you. To have classroom management operate in how you teach and in how your class works, the definition must be yours. Only then can you plan for classroom management, implement a CMP, and reflect on its improvement.

When you respond to question #1, record what classroom management means to *you*. Be careful not to let the literature or others cloud your true thoughts on what this term means to you. Also think about those classroom management skills Heide refers to that teachers need to create and maintain a learning environment. Which of these skills do you possess? Which skills do you wish to improve upon? Do you agree with Heide's definition?

Next consider Shreve's description of classroom management. In what way is your response similar? In what way does your response differ? As an observer, what would you expect to see and hear in Shreve's classroom? How does your classroom compare with your image of Shreve's classroom? Do you wish any of these aspects were operating in your classroom? Why? After envisioning Shreve's classroom, has your definition of classroom management changed at all?

2. Reflect on your philosophy of education. Write five "I believe" statements about teaching.

Jack, who has been teaching high school chemistry for five years, answered in the following way: "1. I believe that as a teacher I should act as a coach, helping my students find the answers on their own, not feeding them the answers. 2. I believe teaching is the single most important profession, and I should strive daily to ensure my students know I feel this way so they respect the profession as well. 3. I believe students can instruct each other, sometimes better than I can instruct them, so group activities are valuable. 4. I believe that a student who feels respected, heard, and cared for will learn better and be better than a student who feels like a number in a grade book. 5. I believe that to teach people well, you must have an understanding of how people learn, so it is important to stay abreast of theories of cognition."

The purpose of this activity is to remind you why you wanted to become a teacher and what you hoped to bring to the profession. Many teachers became teachers because of a teacher they once had. That teacher made a difference in their lives and the lives of other students. Perhaps this teacher made learning fun or was someone who showed students how much he or she cared about them. Teachers begin their careers with a goal to be like their favorite teacher, a strong commitment to the profession, and a passion to make a unique difference. But amid all the classroom responsibilities and with the passage of time, these aspirations, along with remaining true to their teaching selves, get placed on the back burner and sometimes even forgotten.

Reflecting on teaching and writing the "I believe" statements put these goals back into focus and reaffirm priorities. The "I believe" statements reflect who you are and who you can be as a teacher. These statements define your teaching self and can establish your role in planning and implementing classroom management when you incorporate your beliefs throughout the CMP in the ideas, strategies, and behaviors you choose. After writing the "I believe" statements, ask yourself how you can make sure they are reflected in your classroom. Find places in the CMP to address the "I believe" statements. They may appear in the class motto, the rules, procedures, and cues, your lesson plans, the instructional strategies and grading scheme you choose, even in how you use reflection time.

Jack's statement, "I believe that a student who feels respected, heard, and cared for will learn better and be better than a student who feels like a number in a grade book," might be found in his CMP under a class rule such as "Respect must be earned and must be mutual." It might also appear under consequences, where he requires students to complete a behavior log before punishment; under routines and procedures, where he has planned ways students can seek help by holding once-a-week help sessions, using a "buddy" system, holding class meetings, and taking the class climate with a daily or weekly survey; under teaching practices, where he lets students use a "pass or play" option during question-and-answer sessions, where he outlines his responses for partially correct answers as well as incorrect ones, and where he plans student-success strategies; and under evaluation, where his grading plan encourages extra effort because he allows extra credit and rewrites and he averages grades on two or more assignments.

Making sure your CMP reflects your beliefs makes the plan easier to implement and makes its outcome more satisfying. The CMP helps you be who you are and who you want to be in the classroom.

As you read Jack's "I believe" statements, ask yourself what you would expect to see and hear in Jack's classroom. Do you agree with all Jack's "I believe" statements? Are any similar to what you have written? Identify the similarities.

3. List your strengths.

Include both personal strengths and talents. Circle those that apply to classroom teaching.

4. Interview family members.

Ask several family members and friends to tell you what they like best about you, and list their responses below. Circle those that apply to teaching, and note responses similar to yours.

5. List your weaknesses. Circle those the CMP may need to support in question.

Dawn has been teaching kindergarten for three years. Under strengths in question #3, she listed the following: assertive, tactful, caring, understanding, good listener, honest, open-minded, efficient, nonjudgmental. In addition, she added that her love of music—singing and piano playing in particular—is also a strength. She circled all her answers, believing they all apply to teaching.

When Dawn asked her family to tell what they like best about her (question #4), their responses included the following: nice, delightful personality, happy, and a winning smile.

Under weaknesses in question #5, Dawn wrote that she gets discouraged too easily, she is sometimes too sensitive, she can't say no, she tends to run herself dry by giving too much, and she can be impatient.

In developing her CMP, Dawn can capitalize on these identified strengths and find ways to support the weaknesses. She can use the information from questions 3 and 4 in getting to know herself better and learn how others see her. Consider the case of a preservice teacher who in her education classes was a happy, positive, friendly person. This made it all the more surprising when her professor observed her in the classroom and found her a stern, very negative, and unapproachable teacher. The teacher was unaware of the personality switch. It takes a toll being someone and something you are not.

Dawn listed assertive as her first strength. She must ask herself, "What do I mean by assertive? How do I apply this strength in my classroom?" When she views what her family likes best about her, Dawn will see that it is not her assertiveness they mention but that she is a nice, happy person with a winning smile and personality. Dawn may need to get in touch with who she is in a classroom.

Your strengths must carry over into the classroom and be felt by the students. Dawn's CMP can reflect her strengths of being happy and nice and having a winning smile: it might include "Greeting the students at the door each morning," which would be a great way for Dawn to offer the winning smile and transmit her happy attitude to students, parents, other teachers, and all school personnel. She can display her positive attitude in the room decor, the class motto, and her relationships with students and parents.

Dawn also says she gets discouraged quickly, is too sensitive, can't say no, gives too much, and at times is impatient. The CMP can support her perceived weaknesses. To prevent discouragement from setting in, Dawn needs to plan reflection time weekly and, possibly, daily. During reflection, Dawn can start with the positive events that happened, then isolate one or two areas to work on, devising some strategies to try. Reflection can keep Dawn from feeling discouraged and allow her see the bright side to classroom teaching.

Dawn can plan "canned" responses to those who make demands on her time to prevent getting overly involved and committed. Giving too much is a problem for most teachers. So much needs to be done, but they can regulate the timing of getting it all done. For example, Dawn may find calling parents at the beginning of the year a time-consuming task, but she can plan in her CMP how to get the calling done. She might phone the parents of just five students each week for the first five weeks of class to introduce herself instead of attempting to call all of them the first few days or the first week of school.

To support her feelings of impatience, Dawn could note when those feelings occur and plan into her CMP a procedure that eliminates this situation from happening over and over again. For example, if not getting students' attention is a source of her impatience, Dawn could create a cue that gets their attention quickly without her saying a word. If she gets impatient because she has to give directions over and over, Dawn could set up a direction-giving procedure. Maybe she finds herself becoming impatient at the end of the day; she could plan a fun activity she enjoys or read to students to end the day.

6. List the most important qualities you wish to foster in your students.

Kimberly, a preservice teacher, explains, "When I started the courses in education, I was unsure of my choice. I did not like school when I was young. I do, however, remember one good thing about school. I had one teacher who made me want to learn. She was interesting, fun, understanding, and strict all at the same time. Everyone loved her. Maybe we all knew she had a genuine in-

terest in all of us. I am no longer unsure of my career in teaching. I know I want to reach those children who hate school. I want to give them something good to remember. I want to teach to reach a child who is just like I was."

Whether your goal is general—I want to foster in students a lifetime love of learning—or specific—I want students to see that physics is fascinating and fun!—look for ways to build that goal into your CMP. Perhaps under Instruction, you will devise lesson plans that show students they already know more about physics than they realize (Did they know inline skates work by means of friction and inertia?). Or by using the Internet to communicate with a classroom in Norway, your students will want to learn more about geography, languages, and the people and cultures of other lands throughout the world. If your goal is for students to be good citizens of the world, develop rules that teach them respect, honesty, and tolerance.

Identifying possible strengths and weaknesses in others sometimes helps one see inside oneself. Reflect on Kimberly's statement, and list some possible strengths and weaknesses of this teacher. Then evaluate your response to this question. Do you perceive strengths you can capitalize on or weaknesses requiring support?

7. How do you introduce yourself to the class?

Les, a practicing teacher, writes, "For thirteen years, I labored away at an occupation I thoroughly detested. Unhappiness with work finally permeated every aspect of my life. Consequently, at thirty-four years of life, I made a commitment to find a career in which I could completely immerse myself, to enjoy and to love. Already possessing a master's degree, I returned to college at the undergraduate level to complete a teaching certificate. I had correctly sensed that there was no better profession than teaching.

"Teaching has provided me the opportunity to share my love and appreciation for life with others. I am told that the energy I carry into the classroom reverberates off the walls and penetrates the hearts and minds of the students entrusted to me. Magically, they seem to become contagiously wrapped up in my enthusiasm and begin to believe that they can achieve their dreams."

First impressions are very important and no less so for teachers introducing themselves to their class for the first time. Les, the teacher who wrote the preceding statement, likely has a dynamic, exciting way to present his teaching self to his class. Remember the introduction is students' first and, likely, lasting impression. If one of your strengths is creativity, use this strength in your introduction. If you are an athlete or have a special interest or hobby, build that into the introduction. Use props or costumes. Dawn can plan an introduction around her love of singing and piano playing. Kim could share her personal experience of not liking school. The introduction is the ice breaker and the relationship builder.

If you are a preservice teacher, think about how you want your students to regard you in that first impression, then write in detail how you will introduce yourself to the class for the first time. If you are a practicing teacher, consider how you introduce yourself. Do you introduce yourself the same way every year? If yes, do you get the same response every year? Would you like to change students' response? What do you think students think of you? Is this the impression you want them to have? If no, what would you like them to think?

8. Complete a concept map on "What Is Good Teaching?"

Jennifer, the young teacher from the beginning of the chapter, had written a philosophy of education statement while still in college in preparation for employment interviews, but the statement was merely full of theories of cognition and name dropping of key education theorists. She hadn't revised the statement since she'd actually begun teaching and had a class of her own. Jennifer was surprised to learn that Kate fills out the reflection questionnaire at least every two years. When Kate shared her most recent answers, Jennifer found herself nodding in agreement. "That's the way I feel, too, only I don't think I realized I felt that way until I heard you say it." That evening, Jennifer went home and completed the questionnaire. Her concept map looked like Figure 2.2.

Begin the concept map with a circle with "Good Teaching" in the center as in the example shown. List ideas and strategies at the end of spokes that radiate from this center circle. From these, think about how you might accomplish these ideas and concepts and the strategies you might use to do so.

This concept map is a quick way to think about what constitutes good teaching. Use the concept map when writing the CMP. Support the ideas, concepts, and strategies listed throughout the CMP in your choices of room arrangement, rules, procedures, cues, and so on.

9. Write a brief paragraph on how you make a difference in the lives of your students.

The purpose of this exercise is to reaffirm your role, responsibility, and commitment. Putting these thoughts in writing is somewhat like a contract. Consider incorporating these thoughts into your introduction to the

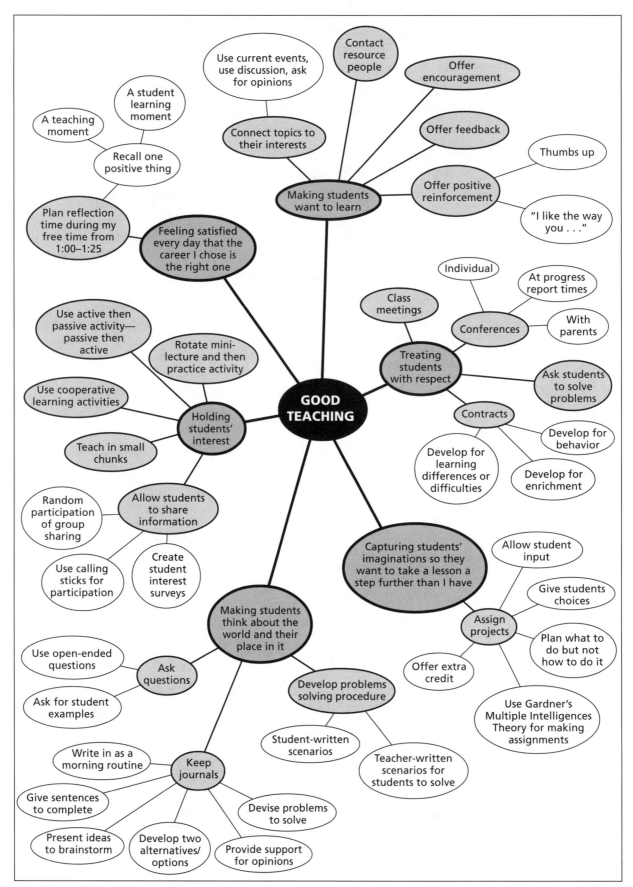

FIGURE 2.2

class or into a class motto such as Make a difference! The answers to this activity can shed some light on why teaching is important, and the CMP takes on more significance because it becomes the tool for making a difference.

10. Find and write a favorite quote, poem, or story that conveys an understanding of your teaching self.

The purpose of this activity is to take something away from this exercise that serves as a tangible reminder to keep in touch with your teaching self. Many people have favorite quotes, stories, poems, sayings, songs, verses, and memories that provide inspiration, motivation, challenge, comfort, encouragement, and hope. People keep them on their desks or walls, in journals or on the pages of a lesson plan book, or folded and tucked in a special place, billfold, or drawer. The purpose of finding the quote, story, poem, saying, or song is to inspire you to stay on the path and feel good about your teaching self and each teaching day.

For Further Reflection

From the point of view of an observer to your classroom, write the ideal observation. What would you like a "review" of your classroom to say? How close is your classroom to this ideal?

Take each aspect the review mentions. Place a star next to those statements you feel you have achieved and an observer visiting your classroom tomorrow would note. Place an X next to those statements an observer might see on a good day or aspects you've experienced but not consistently. Place an O next to those observations an observer to your classroom is not likely to make. Why do you think this item does not exist in your classroom? What steps might you take to have this occur in your classroom? Think about how you might construct your CMP to promote these events in your classroom.

Reflection as an Ongoing Process

As Jennifer learned in the prologue to this chapter, reflecting on past experience and present goals is important and necessary. Whether this reflection takes the form of solitary journal writing or conversations with colleagues, teachers should devote a portion of their day and their week to taking stock of the successes and failures in their classroom, both those of instruction and management. Success breeds more success, and failures (problems) left unattended grow. Teachers need to celebrate effective teaching and learning successes to maintain job satisfaction, but a vital part of effective teaching is being a reflective teacher, a learner, a problem solver, an experimenter, and, always, a student of the art and science of teaching and learning.

Jennifer also learned that reflection is an ongoing process throughout one's career. Such reflection improves teacher effectiveness and learner success. Understanding and reflecting on your teaching self creates opportunities to stay mindful of who you are in a classroom and who you want to be in a classroom and why. Only then can the CMP become the window of possibilities and the conscience of effective teaching and provide you with the impetus to change and the courage to keep trying.

Remember that you will change just as students change. Every year, complete the reflection questionnaire, answering each question again. You may be surprised at how your answers change. The exercise is a way for you to keep in touch with your teaching self and see how your views and values change and how these changes affect the classroom and the way you teach.

Chapter 3

Observation

While his students work in their cooperative learning groups on their lab assignments, ninth-grade biology teacher Cliff Bosler takes a few minutes to take stock of the classroom. At one time, he kept a checklist in the back of his grade book of what to observe, but he has done this now so many times, he no longer needs the list.

He watches as students go from one lab activity to another and gauges the traffic pattern. He confirms that the quiet activities are grouped together in one area while the discussion groups meet in another part of the room near noisier activities. He looks to make sure students have enough room to conduct their experiments—room for all the equipment they need plus room for their notebooks. He checks to see that they have plenty of supplies to repeat experiments if necessary and that additional supplies are accessible to them.

As he moves among the students, he makes mental notes about the experiments that seem to hold their interest longest and most consistently. He listens carefully to their questions, assessing patterns. Is there one experiment all students seem to have difficulty with? Is it a particularly complicated experiment, or are the instructions poorly written?

He watches the interaction among students in the groups in which he has placed them. He makes sure each group member participates in the activity, each performing his or her assigned role such as note-taker or timekeeper.

Cliff uses his time as seventh-period study hall monitor to jot down his observations for the day. Once a year, he supplements his observation with a videotape of the class. The tape allows him to review the class later in depth and with the luxury of distance and time. He keeps these tapes because they provide him with a visual history of how he and his classes change over the years, and he enjoys having a visual record of his students.

The Role of Observation in the Classroom Management Process

Observation is the second phase of the classroom management process. The introspection required in Chapter 2 also prepares teachers to become more acute observers in classrooms, particularly their own. The purpose of this chapter is to help teachers identify specific practices, behaviors, and strategies at work in a colleague's or their own classroom.

The components of a CMP serve as a guide when observing a classroom: classroom management operates through the teaching goal statement, class motto, rules, routines and procedures, consequences, incentives, cues, instructional practices, and teacher and student behaviors. This chapter offers an Observation Guide to help teachers see, hear, and feel what makes a classroom work, talk about why it works, and record how it works. Most observers discover that management can operate unobtrusively in classrooms. The classroom management Observation Guide provides a systematic and focused approach to observing classroom management in a classroom.

An Important Note about Observing a Classroom and its Management

While a definitive definition of classroom management does not exist among those associated with education, many teachers, parents, and administrators base their definition of classroom management on how students *behave* and judge a teacher's effectiveness based on this behavior. A quiet class with students in their seats doing their work suggests to them that a teacher is effective and worthy of a good evaluation. Evaluators are much less likely to expend the effort to judge a teacher's performance on a much more important basis—whether students are learning. For example, teachers seldom use cooperative learning activities if they know they will be observed by a principal. Classrooms will appear noisy and disorganized during cooperative learning activities, and old stereotypes of the ideal classroom are likely to prevail to the detriment of the evaluation.

Observers must learn to evaluate teaching and learning, and the first step to a more meaningful evaluation is to consider "learning noise." All classrooms have learning noise. It is observed readily when students work in cooperative learning situations, read aloud, and help and teach others. Observing learning noise is way to evaluate learning. Learning can be evaluated if a teacher or administrator looks for it, hears it, and feels student "getting it," but they can't do this unless students talk, move around, and think, share, work, and learn together. This chapter asks educators to shed long-held perceptions and move past the stereotype of the appearance of classroom management—desks in rows, students in their seats, no-talking classrooms—and learn to observe classroom management as a process that includes promoting and improving learning.

How to Conduct Observations

Preservice teachers can begin to observe and document the classroom management process during teacher education courses and the early field experiences required in teacher preparation programs. Later they can observe their own classroom as can practicing teachers. Practicing teachers can also look to their colleagues. By observing their own and others' classrooms and using the classroom management Observation Guide to help them focus on the specifics that make up classroom management, teachers can understand that a good classroom doesn't just happen: a plan must be developed that ensures it. Observing practicing teachers who have a classroom management plan provides valuable training for both preservice and practicing teachers, allowing them the opportunity to witness and understand the value of classroom management and obtain ideas to take back to their own classrooms.

Observations can provide many opportunities for professional growth and development. In addition to the Observation Guide, videos and journals can aid the observation process. Often, it takes all these documentation tools to understand fully how the teacher and the class work and how they work together and support each other. While teachers performing a self-observation can complete much of the Observation Guide after they have taught a class, to respond fully and honestly to each of the sections, they should videotape the class. In addition to allowing teachers to observe their classroom more fully and with the luxury of some distance, the video-taping process helps them become accustomed to observers in their room, whether they be colleagues, administrators, or parents.

An additional note on videotaping: Some schools do not allow video-taping of classrooms. Others may allow it if teachers have permission slips signed by parents stating the purpose and use of the tape.

Be Prepared

To prepare to observe a colleague's classroom, follow these guidelines.

• Make several copies of the Observation Guide. Place guides, extra paper, and pencils in a folder or notebook. Read over the guide before the observation so the areas you are to complete are fresh in your mind.

• You will complete the Observation Guide through a combination of observation and interview, so schedule time with the teacher outside of the classroom to clarify certain items and complete those items not exhibited in their classroom such as the teacher's reflection practices.

• Make plans with the teacher to conduct the observations, scheduling the day and time for the observations. Give the teacher a copy of the Observation Guide and explain that you will complete the guide during your visit as many teachers may be concerned about the writing taking place while they are teaching.

• Ask the teacher for a copy of the seating chart and the lesson plan for the day you will visit.

• Ask for a place in the room to conduct the observation that would be least obtrusive and distracting to students.

• During the observation, record information for each component of the Observation Guide. Write in lists and short, incomplete sentences.

• Take time to see, hear, and feel the structure operating in the class-room.

• If you are unable to observe some items, leave them blank. After the observation, discuss the missing items with the teacher.

• Do not limit your observation to teachers who teach the same grade or subject you do. Collect data from teachers of different subjects and in different settings such as primary, intermediate, middle, or secondary grades.

Remember that through observations, teachers can learn both what works and what doesn't. Learning what not to do is as valuable as learning effective classroom management techniques. Equipped with the expertise gained from having seen the modeling of both effective and ineffective teaching, teachers can begin to reach their potential and learn to be effective in any situation, applying whatever a particular classroom needs.

The Observation Guide

This section accompanies the Observation Guide and is designed to help teachers understand what to look for (observe). The information applies to observation of both a colleague's and a teacher's own classroom. The Observation Guide comprises four parts: Observing Classroom Organization (Figure 3.2), Observing Instruction (Figures 3.5 and 3.7), Observing Assessment (Figures 3.8), and Observing Reflective Practices (Figure 3.9).

Overview: The Initial Impression

In *Beyond Discipline: From Compliance to Community*, Kohn suggests that teachers take time in a faculty meeting to define the word *community* in a school context. He suggests that they identify what an observer would see, hear, and feel in a place that is described as a community (1996). The See, Hear, Feel Method of Observation is essentially one's first impression of how a classroom works. Classroom management is *seen* in the room arrangement, bulletin boards, and procedures. It is *heard* in the conversations between teacher and student and among classmates and in the working/learning noise level in the room. It is *felt* in the tone of the classroom—the sense of willingness, positiveness, and encouragement observed or simply the feeling an observer gets being in the classroom (see also Figure 3.1). In the first moments in the classroom, use the See, Hear, Feel Method of Observation, and write what you see, hear, and feel in the classroom.

FIGURE 3.1

First Impressions Count

What first impression would an observer to your classroom have? Reflect on the following statements.

- What would an observer see in your classroom?
- What would an observer hear?
- How would an observer feel about what goes on in your classroom?

Part I: Observing Classroom Organization

1, 2. The first sign of classroom management is in the classroom environment. Much in the physical arrangement either supports classroom management or undermines it. Sketch what you see, including the arrangement of furniture and an interesting bulletin board. If the class has a motto, write it down.

3. Classroom organization is seen next in the formulated policies, rules, routines and procedures, incentives, consequences, and cues. Look for a list of rules, rights, expectations, and/or responsibilities and copy them. If students have classroom jobs, provide some examples. Does a poster or sign identify these students and their responsibilities? In what ways are students recognized in the classroom, for example, student of the week, group of the day, birthday poster. All of this is physical evidence of how the teacher works, how the teacher and students work together, and how the classroom is expected to work.

4. Identify and describe a few observed classroom routines and procedures. Note particularly the routines established when students enter the classroom in the morning or for each bell or period, and the routines for ending the day or each bell or period. What procedure, for example, do students follow when they finish their work?

5. Classroom consequences usually appear on a poster or bulletin board; list them. If you observe consequences, note the amount of time and attention the teacher gives to disciplining a few students in the classroom while the majority of students are waiting to learn.

6. Describe a few individual and group incentives the teacher uses such as no homework if students do well on in-class assignments or free reading time if everyone contributes to a class discussion.

7. Look and listen for democratic ways students can change the structure of the classroom such as through a suggestion board or box, dialogue journals, or scheduled class meetings.

8. Describe the teacher's use of cues to get students' attention, to get order in the classroom, or to signify the beginning of a lesson.

See Figure 3.2 for Part I of the Observation Guide.

Observation Guide

PART I: OBSERVING CLASSROOM ORGANIZATION

Overview: Describe what you see and hear in the classroom and how you feel about what's taking place.

1. Draw or describe the room arrangement and an interesting bulletin board idea.

2. Write the class motto.

3. List the classroom rules as well as rights, expectations, and responsibilities.

4. Describe a few classroom routines and procedures.

5. List the classroom consequences, and describe any consequences you observe.

6. Describe a few individual or group incentives the teacher uses.

7. Describe ways students can change the structure of the classroom.

8. What cues does the teacher use, and how do students respond to them?

FIGURE 3.2
SkyLight Professional Development

Part II: Observing Instruction: Lessons

9,10. Follow the teacher's lesson plan as he teaches. Pay particular attention to the manner in which the teacher teaches and students learn. Observe how the teacher captures students' interest—what "hook" does the teacher use to begin the lesson? Observe how the teacher engages students in the lesson and how he informs students of the lesson objectives. Observe how attentive students are during the lesson and how actively involved and engaged they are in learning the lesson.

11. Describe instructional strategies the teacher uses; for example, does the teacher use themes, graphic organizers, or think-pair-share, guided practice, or cooperative learning activities (see also Figure 3.3)? If the teacher uses such strategies, provide details. If the teacher uses cooperative learning activities, how are the pairs or groups selected? Guided practice is any assignment for which students summarize what they know, write an example, or complete an exercise to practice what they have learned.

12. How does the teacher ensure that all students participate in the lesson? On the seating chart, place an X on students who are called on to answer questions during the lesson. Note students who are called on the most and which students are not called on at all. Write your conclusions. If student response is unequal, reflect on why this might be the case. What could a teacher do to ensure all students participate and are called on?

13, 14. Observing how teachers question students and how students respond provides clues to how well students understand the topic or lesson. Record a few questions the teacher asks students during the observed lesson, and provide examples of how the teacher responds to a student in the following situations: when a student gives a correct answer to a question, when a student gives a partially correct answer, when a student gives an incorrect answer. Record how much time the teacher gives students to answer a question; see Figure 3.4.

15. In explaining how the teacher gives directions to the class, try to identify a consistent direction-giving procedure or pattern the teacher uses. Provide examples of any advanced organizers (use of such terms as *first, next, then, finally*) the teacher uses when giving directions.

16. What techniques does the teacher use to monitor student learning during a lesson? For example, does she stop periodically to question students about what she's taught? Does she scan the room for body language signals from students? Does she walk around while students are working to see if they understand the assignment? Consider also any opportunities the teacher provides for individualized instruction or enrichment to meet the

FIGURE 3.3

Cooperative Learning

Cooperative learning is an instructional strategy that uses student groups to achieve learning goals. The idea is that as a group students can learn more and in less time than they could alone. In addition, the act of teaching each other results in increased understanding and retention. The strategy creates a more cooperative classroom because students must work together to achieve a desired outcome. As a result, they also acquire responsibility, self-esteem, and higher-level thinking, problem-solving, and social skills.

Many different types of instructional strategies fall under the general heading of cooperative learning. The idea underlying all cooperative learning activities is that group members work through an assignment until all group members understand and complete it successfully. All group members gain from the other members' efforts, and the group's success depends on every member's performance. Group members learn to depend on each other, and each rises to the occasion, recognizing that they can achieve their objectives only if each member of the group achieves his or her goal.

One popular cooperative learning technique is the think-pair-share strategy. It consists of three steps. In the first, students think about a question the teacher proposes; second, they discuss their thoughts with partners; and, third, the pair shares their combined thoughts with the class.

Another common cooperative strategy is the jigsaw, in which each group member must teach the other members of the group a particular piece of information, either teacher-supplied or student-obtained. For example, the lesson objective might be to learn nine new vocabulary words. The teacher gives each member of a three-person group three words and their definitions. Each group member teaches the rest of the group his or her three words so by the end of the activity, students know the definitions for all nine words.

Cooperative learning teams are usually mixed by ability, motivation, even sex and race. Cooperative learning needs rules and expectations for working and learning together; procedures for selection of group members and roles for members within the group; a direction-giving procedure for clarity of purpose and quality of work; time limits for efficiency; and evaluation for accountability and productivity. Teachers can add incentives to cooperative activities by giving group points for achievement and improvement on individual evaluations.

FIGURE 3.4

Patience Is More than a Virtue

Response time, or wait time, is the time teachers allow for students to answer a question. Each learner is entitled to time to think before responding to a question. Research indicates that on average teachers wait only one second for a student to respond to a question before the teacher answers the question or calls on someone else (Rowe 1974). Tobin (1987) reports that when teachers' wait time was greater than three seconds, students reached higher cognitive levels of learning. Jones and Jones (1995) suggest that a teacher wait at least five seconds. They cite Rowe who reports that when teachers increase their wait time, the following advantages can occur: length and variety of students' responses increase, failure to obtain a response decreases, students' confidence increases, teacher-centered teaching decreases, and lower-achieving students contribute more (Jones and Jones 1995). To compute response time, count slowly and silently "1,000, 2,000, 3,000 . . ." after asking a question.

---

needs of specific learners in the classroom, and describe opportunities the teacher provides for students to evaluate their own work, note progress, and plan for improvement.

17. What are some success-building strategies the teacher uses? For example, does the teacher hold review sessions before tests? Does the teacher have students keep all their work in portfolios then assess student improvement?

18. On the seating chart the teacher has supplied, use arrows to sketch the teacher's movement during a lesson. Place a square around the spot the teacher occupies most often or returns to as he moves around the room. Are there some areas in the classroom that remain untouched by the teacher's travels? Does the teacher favor one area of the room? Determine if there is a pattern to the teacher's movement. Reflect on how this information can benefit teachers.

19. Closure to a lesson has a purpose just as the opening does. The teacher should ask students to summarize what they have learned. How does the teacher encourage students to provide closure?

20. List the media, visual aids, and resources the teacher uses in the lesson. If the teacher uses the computer in the lesson, describe how. If the school has a computer lab, how does the teacher use the lab? How does the teacher use media, visual aids, and resources in the teaching of lessons?

See Figure 3.5 for Part II of the Observation Guide.

Observation Guide

PART II: OBSERVING INSTRUCTION: LESSONS

9. What "hook" did the teacher use to begin the lesson and capture students' interest? Was the hook effective?

10. Explain how the teacher makes lesson objectives clear to students.

11. Describe instructional strategies the teacher uses that you found effective.

12. Do all students participate in the lesson? On the seating chart, place an X on students called on to answer questions during the lesson.

13. Record a few questions the teacher asks students during the observed lesson, and provide examples of how the teacher responds to student answers.

14. Record how much response time the teacher gives students to answer a question: approximately _____ seconds.

15. Explain how the teacher gives directions to the class.

16. How does the teacher monitor student learning during a lesson?

17. What success-building strategies does the teacher use?

18. On the seating chart, sketch the teacher's movement during the lesson.

19. How does the teacher close a lesson?

20. Describe the teacher's use of resources.

FIGURE 3.5

Part II: Observing Instruction: Effective Teaching Practices

21. Provide some examples of praise. If the teacher uses the positive ripple effect, give an example. The positive ripple effect described by Kounin (1977) is heard in teacher responses such as, "I like the way the class, such as classmates Kathy, Jimmy, and John to name a few, has notebooks on the desk and all are ready to begin." Students hear that and quickly open notebooks and look ready to begin. How does the teacher offer encouragement to students?

22. When observing and recording examples of how students talk to the teacher and each other, note the presence of positiveness or negativity.

23. Describe the oral and written feedback the teacher gives to help students improve the quality of their work or effort.

24. If the teacher uses eye contact and proximity to stop inappropriate behavior, describe the teacher's actions (see also Figure 3.6). If the teacher ignores some behavior, describe a situation. How does the teacher foster student self-discipline and self-control?

25. How does the teacher demonstrate high expectations for student learning? For example, high expectations are seen in the teacher's body language (nodding of head with a wink) and nonverbal signals such as cues (thumbs up); heard in how the teacher asks questions and responds to answers—are the questions stated positively? Do the teacher's responses to students' answers instill confidence? Listen for statements like "I know you can do the job!"

26. Interview the teacher to learn how she promotes positive relationships between herself and students, among classmates, and with parents. Listen for ideas such as get-acquainted activities, interest surveys, and student conferences. Try to determine how the teacher shows how she cares about the students and how the students know the teacher cares.

Note when observing the classroom whether students get along and work together well. Some classrooms are filled with tattling, name-calling, negative remarks, and competition. In an effective classroom, an observer sees less competition, more cooperation, student smiles, and supportive remarks. Comradery, (group) cohesiveness, cooperative spirit, and a sense of community are the four Cs to positive relationships among classmates, and relationship building is the fourth R in classrooms. Listen for the teacher's responsiveness to working with parents. Ask the teacher what strategies have worked in reaching parents and gaining their support.

27. How does the teacher develop students' social skills? Many teachers teach lessons on social skills. They may lead discussions, make assignments, and have guest speakers talk to the class about skills needed to be

---

FIGURE 3.6

Preventive Discipline Strategies

The use of eye contact and proximity are preventive discipline strategies, techniques teachers use to keep situations or problems from starting, continuing, or escalating. Kounin discusses "withitness" and "overlappingness" as two important prevention skills used by effective teachers (Charles 1999). Withitness is anticipating what will happen before it happens; it is noticing, being aware and perceptive, having intuition—in essence, picking up on situations early. Teachers can demonstrate their awareness of classroom situations, their withitness, first with eye contact. The degree of eye contact can range from scanning the room to a prolonged stare while they continue teaching to stopping, staring, and waiting. Next, teachers can use proximity: they close the space between themselves and the problem or situation, moving into the student's space.

Withitness is also collecting information to use later. For example, a teacher displaying withitness might say, "Johnny, that is the second time this week you have not completed your homework." Students recognize that the teacher knows and remembers. Jotting notes and keeping lists help teachers be more "withit."

Overlapping skills are also important for practicing prevention in the classroom. "Overlappingness" is the ability to do more than one task at a time and be in two places at the same time. An example of this skill is monitoring four groups at a time or assisting one group while answering an individual's question. To enhance overlappingness, teachers should position themselves where they can keep the majority of students in view, scan the room frequently, move around the room, plan assistance procedures for projects and assignments, and teach students problem-solving strategies.

---

successful, or they may read books to the class to stimulate discussions on areas of classroom relationships that need development.

28. Do students display any problem-solving or decision-making skills? Do they seem to follow a procedure to solve their problems or make more informed decisions?

29. Does the teacher regularly hold a class meeting? When and how is it conducted? Ask to observe such a meeting, or discuss with the teacher what takes place at the meeting.

See Figure 3.7 for the second half of Part II of the Observation Guide.

Observation Guide

PART II: OBSERVING INSTRUCTION: EFFECTIVE TEACHING PRACTICES

21. Give examples of how the teacher praises and encourages students.

22. Observe and record some examples of how students talk to the teacher and each other.

23. Give examples of feedback the teacher gives students.

24. How does the teacher respond to disruptive behavior?

25. How does the teacher demonstrate high expectations for student learning?

26. Identify the strategies the teacher uses to develop and promote positive relationships with students, among classmates, and with parents.

27. What strategies does the teacher use to develop students' social skills?

28. Describe any problem-solving or decision-making skills students display.

29. Does the teacher regularly hold a class meeting? When and how is it conducted?

FIGURE 3.7

Part III: Observing Assessment

30. Describe the teacher's grading plan. For example, does she use a numeric grading scale? What weight does the teacher assign to certain activities? Do students have input in the grading plan? Does student effort affect the grading scheme? (When assessment is responsive to students and their effort, students demonstrate more effort and thus learn more.) What opportunities do students have to affect their grades? Can students rewrite a paper, and how does the rewrite affect the initial grade? For example, are the two grades averaged? Is extra credit possible? Does the teacher grant students extra time to complete an assignment under certain circumstances? Ask the teacher if you can see the grade book. A teacher may indicate grades in one color, quizzes in another. Also, if a teacher allows students opportunities to impact the grade, the recording of this must be clear and orderly in the grade book. Look for the homework policy, which may be posted, or discuss the policy with the teacher. What is the policy? Do students receive points for homework or outside tasks that can affect a grade? How much does homework count in the final grade? When and how is it collected? When is it considered late? If students have done it but forgotten it, when is the last time to get it in to the teacher and still receive credit? Can students make up homework, tests, or quizzes if they are absent, and how long does a student have to make up the assignments?

31. Does the teacher issue progress reports? Explain the procedure, and ascertain the role of progress reports in the classroom. Does the progress report provide feedback to a student, or is it just a school requirement? Does the teacher use the progress report as an opportunity to discuss the progress with the student and share ideas that may help a student change the situation?

Do students receive an update of grades intermittently for self-assessment and self-monitoring? For example, are students able to view all the grades, check to see if any assignments are missing, and make sure if the teacher recorded the grades for each assignment correctly? Students can then see where the grades went up or down, see how the teacher arrived at the progress report grade, and do the math themselves to calculate and check the teacher's progress report grade.

32. Do students have opportunities to impact their grades by doing extra credit, rewriting papers, dropping a grade, completing special assignments, or other means? Do students receive points for cooperative learning activities or projects that the teacher factors into the final grade?

See Figure 3.8 for Part III of the Observation Guide.

Observation Guide

PART III: OBSERVING ASSESSMENT

30. Describe the teacher's grading plan.

31. Does the teacher issue progress reports?

32. Do students have opportunities to impact the grades?

FIGURE 3.8

Part IV: Observing Reflective Practices

33. Does the teacher schedule time during the school day or week to reflect on what went well and what areas need to be improved? Explain.

34. How does the teacher reflect on classroom and student problems, situations, and experiences? Does the teacher plan time to meet with other teachers who teach at the same grade level or the same subject? If so, how often do they meet? For how long? What sort of topics do they discuss? Does the teacher keep a journal? If so, how often does the teacher make an entry? What might an entry cover?

35. Does the teacher videotape his or her lessons periodically for self-evaluation or peer review? How does the teacher feel about videotaping?

See Figure 3.9 for Part IV of the Observation Guide.

Observation Guide

PART IV: OBSERVING REFLECTIVE PRACTICES

33. Does the teacher schedule reflection time?

34. How does the teacher reflect on classroom and student problems, situations, and experiences?

35. Does the teacher videotape the class for self-evaluation or peer review?

FIGURE 3.9

Chapter 4

Developing a Personal CMP

Kneeling between the rows of newly planted seeds and starts, Mary Williams inserted the last tomato plant in the hole she had dug, sat back on her heels, and looked over her garden. All she had to do was water the soil and let Mother Nature work her magic. But working in the garden had given Mary lots of time to think, and what she had thought about was her first year of teaching, which had ended a few weeks before. It had been an exciting year, a challenging year. She had loved her third-grade class at Wright Elementary, and except for a few minor incidents, she had thoroughly enjoyed her first year. Wright's principal, Bill Phillips, had visited her class several times, and in their meetings that followed his observations, he had both compliments and suggestions for improving her class. In their last meeting, Bill told her he was confident that many of the minor problems he saw would improve as she gained experience. Her style was engaging, he said, her lessons held students' interest, but her group work was weak, and she seemed undecided about the best way to handle disruptive behavior, perhaps, he said, because it was so infrequent.

But he was right. She was still not comfortable with cooperative learning activities, and she wasn't good at handling behavior problems. They threw her and she felt herself losing confidence when such problems occurred. What's more, the students seemed to sense her uncertainty. Taking off her gardening gloves, Mary went into the house and pulled out a manila folder from a drawer in her desk. The folder contained information on creating a classroom management plan. When school starts in the fall, Mary thought, I will be ready. And she sat down with pen in hand and began to write her personal classroom management plan.

The Personal CMP

Evertson et al. remind teachers that "Good classroom management doesn't just happen. Smoothly running classrooms where students are highly involved in learning activities and that are free from disruption and chronic misbehavior do not happen accidentally (1989, xi)." Indeed, such classrooms exist because teachers have a plan to make them happen and are prepared to carry out the plan and meet that goal.

When teachers develop a CMP, they integrate classroom management theory and practice into how they teach, how their students learn, and how their classrooms work. The CMP places this theory and practice into a structure teachers can implement in a classroom, emphasizing teachers' strengths and supporting weaknesses. The plan structures their teaching and student learning yet supports teacher and student autonomy and promotes a sense of community. The CMP maximizes instructional and learning time and minimizes interruptions, distractions, and disruptions. Classroom management, instruction, and teacher behavior interact to create a productive and positive learning environment (Brigham, Renfro, and Brigham 1994).

The CMP reflects teachers' personality, experience, and skills and includes their own ideas, ideas and practices they have observed in effective classrooms, ideas they have read about in textbooks and professional journals, ideas from education courses, and ideas colleagues have shared. Teachers can learn from others, but they can't adopt someone else's teaching or managing style; teachers must write their own script. Educator Les Fortune writes: "Ultimately, a teacher's classroom management style must become an extension of that educator's personality and philosophies combined with the chemistry of the students in the classroom. What works for one may not work for another." Merging the information from the introspection component in Chapter 2 and the observed information from the Observation Guide in Chapter 3, the teacher can begin to develop a personal classroom management plan (Figure 4.1). The CMP can now be personal, realistic, and filled with meaningful content and insights. Teachers can maintain their plan easily throughout the year because it supports who they are and what they want to be in a classroom.

Composing a Personal CMP

Getting Started

Collect the information recorded in chapter 2 as well as the Observation Guide(s) completed in chapter 3. Check or highlight all the items you want to include in the CMP. Look for ideas and strategies that complement your strengths and support your areas of weakness. For example, if discipline is not your strength, stress incentives in your plan. Choose only the consequences you believe you can implement consistently. If you are the type of person who gives second chances, choose a more liberal grading scheme. If you do not want to take time away from lessons to take roll or lunch count, plan the student jobs so students complete these tasks. If you thrive on organization, set up many routines, procedures, and policies for a scheduled, predictable day.

If you are a practicing teacher, your completed CMP may partially reflect what already goes on in your classroom. In other words, if you feel your classroom incentives work well, simply fill in the CMP with incentives you use currently. If you are a preservice teacher, fill in the CMP as if you are describing your classroom, even if it's only as it exists in your mind, using present tense. The following guidelines and questions will help you respond to each component of the CMP and understand how and why this component works. Note the guidelines and questions are in present tense. For all teachers, describing your classroom in present tense helps you internalize your goals and see them as taking place today rather than in some uncertain future time.

Teaching Goal

The plan begins with a teaching goal. Look over the information recorded in chapter 2 for help writing this goal. Your teaching strengths, how others see you, your "I believe" statements, qualities you want to foster in your

My Personal Classroom Management Plan

Teaching Goal:

CLASSROOM ORGANIZATION

Classroom Environment

Draw or describe room arrangement

Sketch bulletin board ideas

Class motto

Classroom Operation

Rules

1.

2.

3.

4.

5.

FIGURE 4.1

My Personal Classroom Management Plan

Routines and procedures

Consequences

1.

2.

3.

4.

5.

Incentives

Cues

FIGURE 4.1 (continued)
SkyLight Professional Development

My Personal Classroom Management Plan

INSTRUCTION

Lessons

Instructional strategies

Individualized instructional strategies

Questioning strategies

Examples of questions

Responses to students

    When a student gives a correct answer

    When a student gives a partially correct answer

    When a student gives an incorrect answer

Student self-evaluation opportunities

FIGURE 4.1 (continued)

SkyLight Professional Development

My Personal Classroom Management Plan

Effective Teaching Practices
Building positive relationships
Between teacher and students

Among classmates

With parents

Strategies to develop student social skills

Strategies to develop student problem-solving and decision-making skills

Strategies to develop student self-control

Preventive discipline strategies

Classroom technology plan

ASSESSMENT

Grading Plan
Recording grades in the grade book

FIGURE 4.1 (continued)
SkyLight Professional Development

My Personal Classroom Management Plan

Homework policy

Progress reports

Student opportunities to impact grades

Extra credit

Rewrites

Drop a grade

Special assignments

Collection of points to be factored into the final grade

REFLECTION

FIGURE 4.1 (continued)

SkyLight Professional Development

students, how you plan to make a difference in the lives of students you teach, and the quote, poem, or story you chose to reflect your teaching self all factor into this goal. Write the goal as one you want for yourself or for your students. This teaching goal sets the stage for developing other ideas in the CMP. For the time-being, keep it a short-term goal—what you hope to accomplish this year, for example. Your goal may be specific—perhaps to focus on instructional strategies that appeal to alternate style learners or to improve your relationship with parents. Or your goal may be more general—to let your students know how important they and their education are, for example.

Classroom Organization

Classroom Environment

Part of classroom environment involves not only making students feel comfortable and safe physically, it includes an atmosphere that makes them feel emotionally secure and valued as persons. Students need to feel accepted and encouraged. They need to feel it's okay for them to take risks. They also need to feel respected and feel their opinions and ideas are worthwhile.

One goal of the CMP is to engender a sense of community in the classroom, promoting and reinforcing positive actions and interactions so a cohesive, supportive group results. Classroom management is seen, heard, and felt in how a class gets along—how pleasant and respectful they are to each other (see Figure 4.2). This sense of community should extend beyond classroom walls to include parents. Classroom management is found in the relationship and developing trust between the teacher and his or her students, among classmates, and with parents. For teachers, students, and parents to be working partners, teachers must develop, nurture, and maintain a feeling of mutual respect, a positive rapport, and a cooperative spirit. Classroom management can't be autocratic, forced, coerced, or teacher-directed; it must be democratic, desired, nurtured, and teacher-student–centered. It is a participatory approach with teacher, students, and parents working together and sharing the responsibility to make the class work efficiently and effectively with positive outcomes—student success and teacher and learner satisfaction.

Draw or describe the room arrangement

Reflect on classroom seating arrangements and visualize the best arrangement to support teacher and student visibility and movement. As you describe the room arrangement, explain why this arrangement works for you. The key to classroom setup is flexibility: try not to get locked into any one arrangement. Furniture placement and seating arrangements should allow you and students to rearrange furniture easily to suit the activity whether it involves students working independently, in pairs, or in groups.

The ability to maneuver in a room in the most efficient, quiet, and least obtrusive way is an objective for any classroom. Because many classrooms are crowded, teachers must spend time reflecting on the best arrangement. To plan the room arrangement, make a scale diagram first, then place only furniture in the classroom that meets the teacher's and students' needs.

FIGURE 4.2

Reflecting on Classroom Environment

- Write one word that best describes your classroom.
- How do you make sure this is the word everyone goes away with after visiting your classroom?

Remember that a perception or feeling or atmosphere isn't there just because you say so. It takes thought, reflection, planning, and effort. Ensure the perception of the class you desire by incorporating action to make it happen it into your CMP. For example, if you want your class to be inviting, what are you doing to make it inviting?

Sketch bulletin board ideas

Bulletin boards should be eye-catching and colorful. Use some bulletin board space for student work and teacher instructions. Let students know what's coming up both in class and in school by posting announcements about such events as upcoming tests and school social events. If possible, make one board an interactive board relating to what students are working on. For example, while you're involved in individual instruction and have assigned seat work to the other students, they can go to the board for activities such as card games, worksheets, and so on. If you teach older students, one board should focus on current events. Post photos of people in the news and have students identify them for extra credit, or staple news clippings on the board, too, and have students match the photos with the news story. Put the class motto on the board (see Figure 4.3). Let students create a bulletin board and change it often to give them a role in how the classroom looks.

FIGURE 4.3

Inspire Students with a Class Motto

Some examples of class mottos:

Attitude makes the difference!

Do your best to be your best!

Soar with the eagles or swim with the fish, just as long as you move toward your true potential!

"And so shines a good deed in a weary world."—Willy Wonka

Reach for the stars and become one!

Classroom Operation

Day-to-day classroom operation is key to classroom management. Teachers need to consider rules, routines and procedures, consequences, incentives, and cues.

Rules

Together, teacher and students should establish rules for the classroom that prohibit disrespectful behavior and set limits on disruptive behavior. Rules should be based on the principle that all students have a right to learn without such behavior infringing on it. The rules the class establishes provide structure to the classroom, and consistent enforcement and reinforcement of the rules is paramount. Teachers should be comfortable with the rules and able to enforce them.

Create relatively few rules so students have no trouble remembering them. Explain to them that rules in the classroom are very similar to society's rules: there's room for growth and individuality, and students have a lot of freedom until they impinge on other students' rights or the general learning atmosphere of the classroom.

As part of the democracy of the classroom, teachers must provide a means whereby students can suggest changes in the classroom operation, including the rules. This may be through a suggestion box, student polls or questionnaires, or a student advisory committee that rotates biweekly and helps teachers create and enforce classroom rules.

Routines and procedures

Think about what events take place daily (bell announcing start and end of class, beginning of lesson, taking attendance, journal writing, etc.) and decide what students are to do and how they are to behave at these times.

For example, when the bell rings at the start of class, where should students be and what should they be doing? How do you give instructions so students have no question about the task and its objectives? What do students do when they finish an in-class activity? Are there routine tasks students might take over to give them responsibilities such as taking roll, distributing handouts, keeping time on group activities?

Think about implementing other procedures. For example, upon entering the classroom, students could write the day's learning objectives in their notebook(s). Copying objectives provides students with a brief preview of the day's lessons. It is also a great organizing and study strategy: students can take notes and complete their assignments in their notebooks under the objectives. Or consider giving a math or word challenge, riddle, problem, or game students can work on until class starts and then discuss or solve it as a class.

Consequences

Teachers need to communicate their expectations regarding student behavior. Students shouldn't have to guess at or "test" the consequences. Teachers should discuss consequences with students the first week of class and leave no doubt of the consequences for misbehavior. Once the class decides on rules and consequences, write them down and provide everyone, including parents, with a copy. A copy should also be on display in the classroom as a daily, physical reminder. Students then choose their behavior with full understanding of the consequences, and, one hopes, they choose discipline and self-control. Either way, they know the consequence they end up with was their choice. The use of rules and consequences teaches students that they are accountable for their actions and as a result builds students' feelings of self-reliance and self-respect.

But meting out consequences can take too much class time—time better spent on instruction instead of correction. Teachers must ask themselves how much class time they take to enforce the consequences on a few students. If teachers find themselves spending too much class time enforcing consequences, they must reflect on what to do differently.

It's important to remember that some students might interpret consequences and the time spent enforcing them as attention—negative attention, certainly, but attention nonetheless. Besides getting attention, repeated misbehavior may be a sign of a learning or emotional problem. If the problem seems to be a behavior problem, reflect more on the incentive side of the CMP—the buy-in to choosing good classroom behavior. Think about some preventive strategies such as establishing a better understanding of and rapport with the student, holding a conference with the student and his or her parents, creating a written contract with the student for change, and, perhaps most importantly, allowing the student to offer solutions and both teacher and student making a commitment to follow these ideas.

If the problem stems from a learning problem, consult the learning resource teacher for techniques specific to student needs. For emotional problems, seek support from the resource personnel and school counselor.

Incentives

Individual and group incentives include grades, points, stickers, parties, free time, talk time, and homework passes. A teacher's verbal and nonverbal responses and students' responses to each other, both verbal and nonverbal, also serve as incentives. Nonverbal incentives include pats on the back, thumbs up, sports referee signals, sign language signals, nods, smiles, and winks.

Cues

Cues are facial expressions, body language, signals, codes, and voiced expressions that send messages, serve as reminders, offer encouragement and praise, reinforce activity, maintain effort, indicate the need for change, provide more direction, reduce distraction, discourage escalation of problems, signal disapproval, serve as a reprimand, and give out punishment. Cues teach, reinforce, and enforce classroom management. Some examples of cues are sounding a whistle or bell, snapping the fingers and clapping the hands, and turning lights on and off.

Instruction

Classroom management supports teaching and student learning. Evertson et al. state that "The lesson outcomes you envision will determine your planning goals and objectives, and your plans should reflect these intended outcomes" (1989, 117). Teachers plan lessons by first writing clear objectives. Taking this a step further, teachers with a clearly defined CMP create a learning environment that promotes the desired outcomes of both good instruction and good management.

Lessons

Teachers must ensure lessons suit different learning styles, present lessons in an engaging manner, vary the presentation from lesson to lesson, state objectives clearly at the beginning of the lesson, and close the lesson by asking students to share what they have learned. Teachers who expect students to perform well and meet or exceed their potential provide stimulating lessons that teach students what they need to know and motivate them to want to learn more. Teachers can also inspire students by demonstrating enthusiasm and communicating by their demeanor that they enjoy teaching.

Instructional strategies

The variety of instructional strategies available to teachers are as numerous as teachers themselves. Teachers should sample a variety of strategies, selecting those they feel most comfortable with and those that seem most effective. Teachers should remember, however, that all strategies require practice (see Figure 4.4). Many teachers attempting cooperative learning activities for the first time, for example, often feel they've lost control of the lesson when students work in groups, they have trouble getting students to work productively in groups, they're unsure how to monitor the groups' progress, or they find that students choose their friends to work with and accomplish little. But trial and error is a part of cooperative learning activities. With practice, teachers can become comfortable with group activities through efforts such as assigning students to particular groups, offering incentives, and establishing rules for cooperative learning activities.

FIGURE 4.4

Practice Makes Progress

Traditional classrooms have been mainly individual, independent, and competitive work environments, so interdependent, collaborative, and cooperative techniques need time and practice. Start cooperative learning activities by having students work in pairs, then move from pairs to groups of differing numbers. Try pair activities such as buddy read, dual practice, pair-role-project, pair-confer-report, and think-pair-share cooperative learning activities before moving to group activities such as team-accelerated instruction (TAI), student team achievement division (STAD), cooperative integrated reading and composition (CIRC), and jigsaw I and II.

Don't dismiss an instructional strategy until you've tried it several times. Get feedback from students about what they like and dislike about the strategy. Remember, if you're using group work for the first time, your students may be just as uncomfortable with the process as you are. You may all need time to get used to a new idea and a new practice.

One direction-giving procedure that can facilitate cooperative learning activities or independent assignments begins with the *give and get* method, in which a teacher *gives* out specific and simple directions in steps and *gets* the instructions back by asking students what they are to do. Next, teachers establish a cue to gain students' attention if needed. Then the teacher sets a time limit and explains how he or she will collect and grade the assignment. Finally, the teacher asks if students have any questions. Students must understand this last step is the time to ask questions, not after the activity or assignment begins (Bosch 1991).

Thematic, integrated units of study are an old but revived and exciting approach to teaching several different subjects together under a theme. An example of a current popular theme is the Titanic, a lesson on which could conceivably cover language arts, social studies, science, math, art, music, character development, and computer technology.

Guided practice activities are opportunities for students to practice and learn the information that was taught to them in the lesson.

Graphic organizers help students understand lessons, complete assignments, study for tests, and organize their work. Common graphic organizers are the Venn diagram, mind maps, webbing, and jigsaws.

Assessing students' prior knowledge is vital to the success of a lesson. Getting them to think about a subject by asking them what they already know about it primes them to receive additional information and make a connection between information they already possess and the new information. Previewing texts by asking students to look at chapter titles or subheads is another way to prepare students to receive new information.

As often as possible, tie lessons into real life or conduct a simulation that mirrors real life. During the President Clinton impeachment debate in the House of Representatives, many classrooms conducted their own debate, with students acting as House members and debating the issue with Robert's Rules of Order in effect.

Review examinations after students take them. If everyone in the class missed one question, look closely at the question. Was it a bad question with confusing or tricky wording, or was it bad instruction that made them all miss it?

Success-building strategies are techniques teachers use to increase student participation, effort, and accomplishment. Examples of success-building strategies include holding review sessions before each test to give students a chance to ask questions and to reinforce important aspects of the lessons; giving students an opportunity to respond to assignments in other ways beside writing, such as singing a song, performing a skit, or drawing a poster; initiating student contracts for learning differences, behavior improvement, and enrichment; asking higher-level questions that allow for more than one right answer; allowing students to collect points in classroom games and activities rather than "winning" and "losing"; and recognizing students for achievements other than "A" papers. See Figure 4.5 to reflect on instructional strategies.

FIGURE 4.5

Reflecting on Instruction

- Provide some examples of encouragement you use.
- Record the direction-giving procedure you use each time you give directions to students.
- How do you ensure you give students adequate response time?
- How do you monitor student learning?
- What procedure do students follow when they finish their work?
- List all the ways you select group participants for cooperative learning activities.
- What are your rules and responsibilities for working in groups?
- What are some ideas you have for great beginnings to lessons?
- What are some themes you use to teach integrated units of study?
- What graphic organizers do you use?

Individualized instructional strategies

One individualized instructional strategy is to take an interest inventory: ask the student what kind of activities he or she enjoys. The answer gives the teacher an idea what kind of learner the student is—visual, oral, kinesthetic, and so on—then the teacher can structure activities so they build on the student's multiple intelligence strength and give alternative style learners the opportunity to excel. Another strategy is giving a variety of options for evaluation. For example, for a writing exercise, give students the option of writing several shorter journal entries or one longer essay, performing a skit, or doing an interview, and letting students choose the task that suits their strengths.

Contracts between teacher and student are particularly useful in cases of learning differences, enrichment opportunities, and behavior problems. A contract for learning differences is a program of study determined by teacher and student that may allow more time to complete assignments, fewer problems to complete at one time, different assignments from the rest of the class, and so on. Both teacher and student sign, evaluate, and fulfill the terms of the contract. The behavioral contract is an agreement between the teacher and student to change behavior for more appropriate behavior. The contract is specific with shared expectations, incentives, and consequences for this effort. A contract for enrichment gives students opportunities to extend their learning, complete a project, write a report, draw a map, make a volcano, and so on. The strategies the teacher develops provide opportunities for the student to learn, progress, succeed, gain confidence, and take risks.

Questioning strategies

Questioning is a skill teachers must develop and practice to improve student learning. Questions should enable students to apply prior knowledge and experience to the new knowledge to enhance learning of the material.

Examples of questions

Ask open-ended questions from the cognitive domains of Bloom's Taxonomy. Such questions ask students to demonstrate their knowledge (or memory) and comprehension (or interpretation), then to use their application, analysis, synthesis, and evaluation skills (Bloom 1956). If the subject is the fairy tale *Cinderella*, ask students if they can remember a time when they felt like the main character—an application question. Under evaluation questions ask, if they were the main character, would they have taken the same action? Do they think the character did the right thing? Under analysis, have students list three of the main character's qualities. Then based on what they know of the character, how might the character behave if placed in their town?

Responses to students

Determine ahead of time how you will react to students when they give a correct answer, a partially correct answer, or an incorrect answer. Your response should demonstrate respect for their attempts and encouragement to try again. For example, if the answer is partially correct, you might say, "That's a good way of looking at it." But try not to ask the sort of question that has a definite right or wrong answer. If, however, the subject is math or another subject where the answer is either right or wrong and the student answers incorrectly, you might say, "Let's see how you got that answer."

Student self-evaluation opportunities

Self-evaluation is a way for students to monitor their learning and an opportunity for teachers to foster more student autonomy. Through self-evaluation, students can determine grades, progress, improvement, strengths, areas of weakness, missing assignments, mastery of skills, and skills needing practice. The student spends time observing and collecting information pertaining to these areas. For example, students might make a graph to record their grades on in-class assignments, tests, quizzes, and homework. The graph provides a visual self-evaluation of progress.

Effective Teaching Practices

Effective teaching practices are behaviors that promote learning and create a positive classroom atmosphere (See Figure 4.6). Offering praise and encouragement, providing feedback, and communicating high expectations are specific ways teachers can help create a positive classroom atmosphere. Jere Brophy (1981) reminds teachers that praise has an active role in any classroom. Praise feels good—everyone wants to receive it—and it is an incentive for most. Praise projects approval, agreement, acknowledgment, support, and satisfaction. Praise is expressed in such expressions as "Great effort!" "Super worker," "Terrific day!" "Wow! I like that!" "Good detail, nice word!" "Used a spelling word!" "Interesting!" "Creative!" "You are prepared!" "I like your thinking!" "Your thinking cap is on today!" Some examples of encouragement are "You're on a roll!" and "I know you are thinking about that topic sentence! Good start! Keep it up! Terrific thinking!"

Teachers can offer feedback in oral and written comments and suggestions during guided practice and question and answer sessions and on homework, in-class assignments, progress reports, and notes home to parents. Feedback must be specific and clear and must provide the student with the opportunity to act on it. Some examples of feedback statements are, "This is good. If you add an example it will be excellent!" "Good start on that description of the main character! Can you add two more adjectives?" "You have compared the two characters, now add some contrast." Written feedback on papers offers so much more to a learner than comments such as Vague, Awkward, and Do over! Written feedback includes, "Every paragraph needs at least three details," "Remember to indent when you discuss each new idea," "Research papers need at least five sources, and cite references in the text." Feedback provides information the learner can act upon to learn.

One way of treating students with dignity and respect is to expect them to do well. High expectations are important to student achievement.

Teacher statements and actions can demonstrate this confidence in students or undermine students' efforts. For example, a teacher can demonstrate high expectations by saying, "I know you can do this assignment well," or defeat such expectations by saying, "This is a difficult assignment, probably too hard for most."

FIGURE 4.6

Supportive Strategies

- Provide some examples of how you demonstrate high expectations for student learning.
- Provide an example of how you use the positive ripple effect.
- How do you develop a sense of group cohesiveness, class comradery, and a sense of community?
- How do you help students get involved in community projects?
- What opportunities do you give your students to change how the classroom works?
- How do you conduct classroom meetings?
- What is your strategy to ensure all students in class participate?

Building positive relationships

Relationship building strategies are vital to the CMP development. Teachers need to build teacher-student relationships by planning into the CMP get-acquainted activities, getting-to-know-you exercises, interest surveys, teacher-student conferences, class discussions, and opportunities for student involvement, input, and self-control. Teachers need to provide in the CMP many ways to create, encourage, and reward positive classmate relationships through such ideas as a buddy system, group activities and projects, peer tutoring, and "catch them being good to each other" incentives. Teachers can build into the CMP ways to work with parents such as an introductory letter to parents, making positive phone calls before asking for support, soliciting their help with class activities and needs, keeping them informed by sending papers home once a week, sending home a student-created newsletter, alerting parents early before problems escalate or grades drop, and being accessible to parents by means of phone, e-mail, and posted office hours.

Between teacher and students: Teacher-student conferences, for example, to discuss progress, grades, discipline, or any other topic are a powerful and meaningful strategy to build relationships. Conferences between the teacher and the student open the lines of communication, establish rapport, and help them develop respect for each other. A teacher and student can develop a plan of action—a contract or agreement—to work through areas of concern. Students feel more empowered when it comes to evaluation, and they feel they have more input and control in how the class operates. Holding class meetings on a regular basis in which teachers discuss with students everything that goes on in the classroom from lessons to student behavior to decorations is another valuable way to build relationships. Class meetings also create and maintain a sense of ownership among classmates for the classroom and the way it operates.

Among classmates: Positive student relationships are important to how the class works. Teachers can foster these relationships by giving students many opportunities to work together. Allow students time to get to know each other. Peer tutoring, peer assistance, and even the buddy system are opportunities for students to learn how to work together and learn together. Class activities can bring the group together such as working together on a community or school project, creating a bulletin board, planning school functions, or participating in fairs, a class open house, and science night.

With parents: Keep parents informed about what goes on in the classroom. Send a letter to them at the beginning of the year, making them aware of your goals for the year, and send another letter at the end of the year telling them how much you enjoyed working with their child. Send home letters announcing upcoming units, perhaps asking for parents with expertise in that area to visit the classroom. Notifying parents in advance of a unit of study is particularly important if you are teaching a subject that could be considered controversial. Keep your door open to parents. Make sure they feel welcomed in your classroom. To reinforce the community spirit, include students in parent conferences. Send home a copy of your classroom rules and consequences as well. A student, teacher, and parent create a learning triad—by working hard and giving lots of time, lots of attention, and loads of support, they can see learning achieved.

Strategies to develop student social skills

Teachers may need to teach, review, and reinforce social skills and establish rules of conduct and rules for communicating when students work together. Include classroom texts that contain some social skill emphasis, make assignments that employ social skills and discuss why they are important, and share experiences requiring social skills. Students need opportunities to practice social skills. Include time in the day for nonscholastic discussion to get students to interact in a more social way. Develop scenarios and have students role-play, teach a social skill, or establish dos and don'ts for communication. Create strategies and procedures to assist the class in using social skills. For example, remind students that they will respect each other at all times, even when they disagree. When introducing think-pair-share activities to them for the first time, tell students the primary rule is they must be accepting of others' ideas.

Strategies to develop student problem-solving and decision-making skills

Problem-solving and decision-making strategies support learners in times of doubt, confusion, and frustration and when they have questions or need assistance. For example, one strategy to help students become problem solvers is the 5-Step Unstuck Procedure, which helps a learner having a problem with an assignment: students should first, reread the directions; second, go on to the next problem; third, ask a peer for help; fourth, place a colored index card on the desk to indicate the need for teacher assistance; and, finally, take out other work to do or a library book to read silently until the teacher can help (Bosch and Kersey 1993).

Have the class decide on problem-solving procedures; for example, to resolve the problem of what to do when they have finished their work, the class may decide to choose from the following options: place a Finished card (a colored index card) on the corner of the desk, start other class assignments, read a library book, go to the learning center, or use the computer.

Strategies to develop student self-control

Students with difficulty controlling themselves need to practice self-management techniques. The teacher and the student may decide to create a self-monitoring plan. For example, they focus on one behavior and thoroughly discuss what the student needs to do to practice that appropriate behavior. The student places an index card listing that behavior on his or her desk. The student records with an X the number of times he or she demonstrates this behavior in a day for each day of the week. At the end of the day or week, the teacher and student discuss the student's progress. The student can count and see the Xs on the card that show progress. The teacher can also have the student graph the Xs, then reflecting on the collected data, the student and teacher can see trends and draw conclusions. When the graph continually improves or the number of Xs continues to increase, practice another behavior.

In many classrooms, students go voluntarily to a time-out place to regain composure for an amount of time decided by the teacher or the class. When the amount of time has been served, the student returns to his or her seat. The class can also decide on ways to solve conflicts. For example, if two students are arguing, the class may ask the designated "class lawyer" to listen to the problem. If a classmate fights physically with another classmate, the resolution plan may be to place chairs back to back and have students each take a seat. Each student must tell the class the problem, next, tell how the problem started and how the problem can end. The two students need to decide and then tell the class how they will work together to solve the problem. Among other conflict-resolution plans is choosing a forum to air problems such as class meetings or a class court.

Preventive discipline strategies

Preventing discipline problems requires an attentive and responsive teacher alert to students, their needs, and ever-changing classroom conditions. Teachers must determine what kind of behavior they will ignore and how they will exhibit disapproval to students who misbehave (see Figure 4.7). Body language is quick, effective, and powerful: eye contact and proximity may be all that is necessary to stop inappropriate behavior.

FIGURE 4.7

Reflecting on Discipline Strategies

- What is the first level of disapproval you will demonstrate to the student?
- What kind of behavior will you ignore?
- How will you use eye contact and proximity to stop inappropriate behavior?

Classroom technology plan

The first step in creating a classroom technology plan is determining what resources are available in the classroom. For example, does your room have a television, VCR, tape recorder, computers, headsets? Next, specifically describe how you use technology in the teaching and learning of lessons, and how you use the classroom computer and the school's computer lab.

The use of media, visual aids, and resources shows teacher planning and preparation. Students and others view the use of such resources as extra effort by teachers (see also Figure 4.8). If the teacher is viewed as hav-

FIGURE 4.8

Be "Resource" full

Are art supplies accessible, or do you have to order them from another location in the school? Do you have globes, maps, a set of encyclopedias? What about human resources: do you have aides? Do you team teach? Do you have parents or other volunteers who help out in the classroom?

Think about the classroom resources available in addition to electronic resources. Teachers find that reflecting on the curriculum and its objectives and even some lessons helps them plan better use of resources. The teacher can collect information, search for the information on the Internet, collect supplies from the media room or center, order in advance the tapes, pictures, and materials for the lessons, purchase materials, get related books from the library, plan time with the librarian for use of the library, and sign up for the computer lab. The teacher can ask for resources from other teachers and plan and solicit information and support from parents. Teaching with resources can spark interest and enthusiasm for learning, make content clearer, activate students' prior knowledge, and help meet individual needs for learning based on multiple intelligences and learning styles theories.

---

ing done his or her homework, trying hard to do more not less, and attempting to do the best job possible, this becomes a class norm, value, and expectation. The teacher is modeling a behavior that can be expected from students.

Assessment

The evaluative structure of classroom management must have a two-way communication flow. Too often, students report that grades are what a teacher gives to them. Students should feel they have earned their grades. Grades are earned when the person being graded is given feedback, has some input, and has been afforded opportunities to impact the grade or how the evaluation is conducted. This feeling of empowerment is necessary in gaining students' full participation and commitment to learn, continue learning, and improve their learning.

When assessing students, be sure their work matches the objective of the lesson. Simply put, if you told them to sing a song, they can't dance a dance. Some teachers find creating a contract with students an effective way of giving them input in their grade as well as giving alternative style learners an assessment option. The contract makes goals and objectives of a unit of study explicit; for example, this is the reading unit, and this is what you must accomplish during this unit. Have students sign the written contract. If they don't accomplish the terms of the contract, their grade reflects it.

Grading Plan

Your grading plan represents what you believe about students, teaching, and learning. The plan should be fair and reflect curriculum standards yet be flexible and provide opportunities to improve grades. The plan must be one you can and want to support and consistently apply to classroom assignments and tests. And a grading plan must support the ideas in the CMP.

Recording grades in the grade book

Consider how you will manage the grade book if assignments count for different percentages or you allow students to redo certain assignments in an attempt to improve their grade. How will you note the first grade, then the second? The record of this must be clear and orderly in the grade book. If quizzes count for a certain percentage and tests another percentage, the grade book must display the difference for ease in final calculation of the grade. Most important, students must be allowed to see their grades to monitor their progress. A grade book can paint a picture of a student's effort, ability, proficiency, reliability, and attitude. Grades should not be a secret or a mystery to learners.

Homework policy

For homework to be important and for students to do it, it must impact the grade. Develop a homework policy and teach it. As you write the CMP, consider the following: How much does homework count in the evaluation plan? When and how is it collected? When is it considered late? If students have done it but forgotten it, when is the last time to get it in and still receive credit? How many days do students get to complete homework when absent? Homework that is partnered with a policy and an incentive—the incentive being that it has an effect on their grade—fosters more student involvement, commitment, effort, and practice time for learning.

Progress reports

Progress reports give students feedback and allow them to evaluate their progress or lack of it and make decisions about changing the course of events. Grades, progress, or lack of progress should not be a surprise to the learner. Learners need to know their status and get feedback on how to do better or what to do differently. If students are to be more responsible and accountable for their own learning, teachers must provide an opportunity for them to take and accept more control. Progress reports could do just that if planned as a student opportunity to affect their grade.

Student opportunities to impact grades

Students need to exercise some control over their learning and their grades. Effort must play a greater role in their work for effort equals outcome. Students must have opportunities to affect their grades through such avenues as extra credit, rewrites, dropping a grade, special assignments, and collection of points for cooperative learning activities and independent tasks. These opportunities offer students options and possibilities, then leave it to students to take advantage of them and take charge of their own learning.

Reflection

The final step in writing a personal CMP is reflecting on the content to this point and refining it. Chapter 6 explores teacher reflection in greater detail. In this section, the goal is to reflect on the draft of the CMP.

Making Reflective Connections

First, identify which of the components of the CMP need student involvement and input and, therefore, need to be developed in the classroom. Classroom management that has student involvement creates more student on-task behavior and accountability to classroom teaching and learning. Each class, each year is different, which means the CMP requires new teacher and student input to be effective and relevant.

Second, reflect on each component and connect this information to student needs of belonging, power, fun, and freedom as outlined by William Glasser (1986). A comprehensive classroom plan that provides for students' needs is an important way to prevent discipline problems (Edwards 1997).

Third, reflect on the CMP to integrate its components and ideas. This integration of ideas results in the support of each idea by another idea in another place in the CMP. This support makes it virtually impossible for students not to follow the CMP. When the CMP includes student input, when it meets student needs, and when it weaves support of one idea with another in the plan, students can't help but follow the plan. It just happens!

Reflect on the CMP to include student involvement and input

Allowing students to have a role in the development of the CMP takes time, but the rewards are many. Reflect on the components that need student involvement and input for a more relevant and meaningful CMP such as rules, procedures, cues, and incentives. Take the CMP to the classroom at the start of the school year, and get the needed student input. Change the content in the CMP to reflect the student input.

Reflect on the CMP to connect components to students' needs

Glasser maintains that "all human beings have genetic needs for 1. survival; 2. belonging (security, comfort, legitimate membership in the group); 3. power (sense of importance, of stature, of being considered by others); 4. fun (having a good time, emotionally and intellectually); and 5. freedom (exercise of choice, self-direction, and responsibility)" (Charles 1999). Glasser stresses that teachers must plan to meet these needs in a classroom. He suggests that

> Students sense belonging when they are involved in class matters, receive attention from the teacher and others, and are brought into discussions of matters that concern the class. Students sense power when the teacher asks them to participate in decisions about topics to be studied and procedures for working in the class. A sense of power comes, too, from being assigned responsibility for class duties, such as helping take attendance, caring for class animals, helping distribute and take care of materials, being in charge of the audiovisual equipment, and so forth. Students experience fun when they are able to work and talk with others, engage in interesting activities, and share their accomplishments. And they sense freedom when the teacher allows them to make responsible choices concerning what they will study, how they will do so, and how they will demonstrate their accomplishments (Charles 1999, 151).

Reflect on the CMP to integrate its components and ideas

The last step in making reflective connections is to trace the integration of one component or idea with another component or idea in the CMP. If necessary add ideas to ensure support of an idea from one component to another. The goal is for the ideas in each component to be supported by ideas in another component. For example, if one of the classroom rules is "Be prepared for class," look for support of this rule throughout the CMP (see Figure 4.9).

FIGURE 4.9

Rule #1: Be Prepared for Class

To look for support for the rule "Be prepared for class" throughout the CMP, begin by reviewing the Classroom Organization component. Is this rule supported by a routine or procedure? If a routine or procedure listed in the CMP supports this rule, go to another component and look for support for this rule. However, if no procedure supports this rule, add one to your CMP; for example: when the bell rings, students must have their journals opened, have two sharpened pencils on their desks, and begin their daily journal entry. Students have ten minutes to write. When the bell rings the second time, the row captain picks up the journals and places them in the row bin.

Continue with this reflection by looking at the room arrangement, bulletin board ideas, and the class motto. Do they support this rule? Are incentives linked to the rule? Making these connections strengthens the effectiveness and efficiency of the CMP.

Trace each rule through the CMP. An idea or rule standing in isolation with no support within the CMP usually fails. The integration of components and ideas creates a situation whereby students follow the rules naturally; it is just how the classroom works. Next, look at incentives and see if the plan supports them throughout. Take each component and trace the integration of ideas. Finally, evaluate the integration of the components and the ideas expressed in the CMP. Revise your CMP to reflect this evaluation.

Chapter 5

Implementing the CMP

After their conversation in the teacher's lounge, Jennifer and Kate began meeting each week over coffee to discuss their classes. Tonight, at Jennifer's request, Kate had brought her classroom management plan and a folder full of lesson plans.

"I always thought of classroom management as an idea—you know, an abstract concept," Jennifer said as she looked over the materials Kate had brought. "I never thought about writing a plan for it, making it something tangible."

"I felt the same way," Kate admitted. "In fact, when I first started teaching, I felt a little lost. I knew my subject matter, I liked the kids, but I had trouble managing my classroom time. I would make my lesson plan but never get through it before class ended. There'd be distractions and interruptions, I'd spend far too much time repeating instructions for assignments, or I'd assign seat work so I could meet with students individually, and my students would end up chatting about the upcoming dance or making paper airplanes out of my worksheets.

"Every year students voted Anne Cooper the teacher of the year. And Anne taught math, for heaven's sake! When students vote a math teacher the best of the year, you know she's doing something special. So I asked her if I could sit in on her class. And I was amazed. Her students worked hard, but they seemed to be having a good time, too. I couldn't really put my finger on what she was doing or how, but the atmosphere in her classroom was charged. I met with her after my visit, and she showed me her classroom management plan, and I went home and wrote one up right then and there."

"Do you mind if borrow your plan and these lesson plans for a little while? I'd like to take some time to look them over. I know I can get some good ideas from them."

"Take your time with them."

"But I don't think I could do all of this." Jennifer looked uncomfortable for a moment. "Do you really dress up as characters in history when you teach?"

Kate laughed. "I do, yes. But that doesn't mean you have to. Take from my plan and my lessons anything you can use, but don't expect to borrow from them wholesale. Borrow a little, borrow a lot, but adapt them so your plan and your lessons suit your teaching style and your personality."

"I will!" Jennifer exclaimed with a grin. "I feel like I'm a new teacher again! And I think my students are in for a surprise."

Set the CMP in Motion

Implementation is the fourth phase of the classroom management process. The CMP is now a relevant, comprehensive, and integrative plan to structure classroom management into how a teacher works and how a classroom works.

The first step in implementing the CMP is teaching students the rules, routines and procedures, consequences, and incentives of the classroom. Teachers can teach their CMP along with the curriculum by planning CMP mini-lessons. Depending on whether the lesson is to teach or review the components of the CMP, the lessons may take as long as thirty minutes or as little as ten minutes. Teachers can intersperse the CMP mini-lessons throughout the school day as needed to teach, review, or reinforce areas of the CMP. These CMP lessons are just as important as curriculum objectives, lessons, and goals.

Teachers may express concern about the time required to plan CMP lessons, but planning the mini-lessons can be done in advance of the school year. Preservice teachers can develop mini-lessons in teacher education courses and during their field experiences. Inservice workshops for practicing teachers can provide a planning session for the writing of CMP mini-lessons. Both preservice and practicing teachers can develop the lessons alone or in groups and exchange them with peers. The lessons can be collected and placed in a notebook in the school library and used by all faculty.

Teachers have stated that they have no time in the day to teach additional lessons, that curriculum fills the school hours. Herein lies the commitment teachers must make to their profession. Building classroom management into each school day begins with preparing and teaching the CMP. Preparing the CMP can begin before the first day of school; however, teaching the CMP must begin the first day of school. Evertson stresses that ". . . solving managerial and organizational problems at the beginning of the year is essential in laying the groundwork for quality learning experiences for students" (1989, 90). Wong and Wong maintain that good control of the class needs to be established in the first week of school. Good control is not threats and intimidation but knowing what one is doing (1998).

Planning CMP Mini-Lessons

Teachers need to think seriously about the teaching and learning that take place in the first few weeks of each school year. Much time is spent in review; specifically, teachers try to determine what students know and can apply to the learning of new skills. Streamlining the review that begins every school year not only creates time for teaching the CMP but can reduce the boredom, down time, and segregation of learners based on interest, ability, and aptitude.

The CMP implemented with commitment continually supports more student learning and the rigors of the curriculum. The CMP taught and learned affirms within the teacher and students a sense of pride and ownership for how "their" class works. The CMP ensures a level of teacher and student autonomy, competence, confidence, interdependence, and accountability that is needed in today's classrooms and those of the 21st century.

The number of CMP mini-lessons and the amount of time allotted to teaching each lesson depends on the teacher and the class. Teachers must make decisions based on how they teach the CMP and its components and observing whether students have learned the information. But the CMP should begin to operate on the first day and continue until the last day of the school year.

Effective Lesson Structure

Like all good lessons, the sample CMP mini-lessons in this chapter have four necessary elements: objectives, opener, instruction, and closure (see Figure 5.1). An independent practice activity may also be included.

Objectives

The lesson plan begins with the objectives. Teachers need to communicate the reasons for teaching the lesson to students, and students must understand what they are expected to learn in the amount of time of the lesson. Knowing their respective responsibilities for the teaching and learning of the material of the lesson during the block of time can also keep teacher and students on task. To this end, write the lesson objectives on the board or overhead.

Opener

The second element is the opener. The opener is the first impression, the hook that gets students' attention. It must be interesting, relevant, and engaging. The opener can be a cartoon, story, quote, picture, role-play, and so forth. The opener lasts approximately two to three minutes, five at maximum, and facilitates a smooth transition into instruction.

Instruction

The next element of the lesson is instruction. Teachers need to plan instruction to include both a teaching strategy and a learning strategy for each objective of the lesson. A teaching strategy is how the teacher teaches the lesson and a learning strategy is how the learner will learn, or practice, the lesson. Keeping these two areas distinct in the lesson plan enables the teacher to move from the role of instructor to facilitator. After the lesson, while students are trying out or practicing their understanding of the new information, the teacher becomes a facilitator, circulating around the room helping students and monitoring their understanding.

Monitoring learning can include observing students' willingness to participate, their indecisiveness in responding, their hesitation in starting the assignment, and their difficulty with the assignment. Monitoring requires teacher alertness and attentiveness to the learning needs of stu-

CMP Mini-Lesson

Grade:
Time:
Materials:

Objectives:

Opener:

Instruction:

Closure:

Independent Practice:

FIGURE 5.1
SkyLight Professional Development

dents. It consists of the teacher making eye contact, scanning the room frequently, moving around the room, and noticing student difficulties (see also Figure 5.2). Teachers need to plan monitoring moments or activities in their lessons during which they observe and assess student learning. Monitoring renders results only if teachers plan for it, collect information, then apply this information to their teaching.

FIGURE 5.2

Signs of Uncertainty

Students who don't understand the lesson, information, or directions or who are experiencing difficulty in the guided practice activity unconsciously move their necks forward and squint their eyes in a manner one can call the "learning jerk." Teachers need to monitor students during instruction to recognize the messages they send about their learning. The learning jerk is a telltale sign of individuals needing more instruction or practice learning the information.

If during monitoring the teacher observes students having difficulty learning the information, they can decide to return to teaching and provide more examples, offer more guided practice, or change the teaching/learning exchange.

Three teaching/learning exchanges exist: 1. teacher to students, or direct classroom instruction; 2. student to student, or cooperative learning; and 3. one on one, or individualized instruction. When students experience difficulty, teachers must consider changing the teaching/learning exchange. For example, if students do not understand the material through the first exchange—direct teaching as in a lecture—teachers should try the second level of exchange, which is student to student, students learning from each other in a group, or cooperative setting. This gives students a chance to learn from their peers. If that level doesn't work, teachers can try the third level, which is one-on-one teaching, or individualized instruction.

In addition to monitoring student learning during the teaching of the lesson, they must ascertain the student learning quotient (LQ), the number and names of students who do and don't understand the material divided by the number of students in the class. This percentage gives teachers a sense of what the majority knows, which means if the majority understands, the teacher can and must move on. If less than the majority understands, teachers can provide more teaching and learner practice.

To determine the student LQ, teachers seek answers to the following three questions during the guided practice activity: Who knows, Who doesn't know, and How many know the information? Thus, to collect the LQ, teachers teach to the first objective, assign a guided practice activity, then monitor and assess students' learning. To assess the LQ, teachers might do the following: Give students a problem and two answers to choose from. Ask for a show of hands on those who choose answer #1 and another for those who select answer #2. This exercise indicates quickly who knows the answer. Teachers can also walk around and check students' work, or use a copy of the student roll on which the lesson's objectives are listed. With the roll in hand, teachers can monitor a guided practice activity and record the LQ by placing codes next to students' names: + = mastery of the information, O = acceptable understanding, − = marginal understanding. This information can help teachers teach the current lesson plan, make more appropriate assignments, select group members for cooperative learning activities, and provide individual attention time or peer tutoring for some students. In addition, recording LQ information may help teachers in the reflection process. The LQ information can reveal areas for teachers to reflect on for improved lesson planning and to increase all students' learning.

Closure

The final element in a lesson is closure. An appropriately planned closure allows students to express what they have learned and to realize that they, indeed, have learned something. During the closure portion of the lesson, the teacher listens for what has been taught coming back in student words. Closure can provide learners with confidence that they've achieved the lesson objectives. It also brings purpose to learning. Students who do not have an active part in the closure of the lesson really don't know what they know or have learned. This may be one reason, when asked by teachers or parents what they did in school today, students frequently respond by saying, "Nothing." Or when asked, "How was school?" they say "Boring"— they haven't been set up to give back information. They haven't had the chance to think through their learning. Closure is that chance.

Elementary school teachers should try to provide closure at the end of the day as well as lesson closures. They should ask students what they learned today, or what they can't wait to tell their parent about school today, or what is one thing they think they could teach their brother or sister that they learned today. Then when asked what they did in school that day, students would have something to say because they have had a chance to organize and think about their learning. Their answer would undoubtedly generate a positive response from their questioner, which would make them feel good about themselves and want to learn more.

The Power of Learning

When teachers highlight the objectives for the lesson, plan an inviting opener, monitor student learning during instruction, and provide more student-generated closures, students can be more autonomous, accountable, and empowered in their learning. As Glasser states, "A good school could be defined as a place where almost all students believe that if they do some work, they will be able to satisfy their needs enough so that it makes sense to keep working" (1986, 15). Creating independent learners is one of the goals of schooling. The CMP provides the structure for students to practice autonomy in the classroom and in their learning and be part of a community of learners. Teachers cannot expect students to be independent learners without providing them with opportunities to learn to be more independent and feel the empowerment of knowledge.

Teaching the CMP

The discussions and mini-lesson plans in this chapter have been developed to assist in teaching the CMP to the class. The lessons are designed for a variety of grade levels and require differing amounts of teaching time. CMP mini-lessons may have to be taught more than once to the class, or shorter but more precise classroom management mini-lessons may be needed for review and reinforcement of the plan's components. Teachers must not assume that if they teach a component of the CMP once, students will understand and follow it. CMP objectives need the same commitment to learning frequently brought to curriculum objectives such as review, practice, and reinforcement. Teachers must teach a CMP mini-lesson then assess whether students have learned the lesson and achieved the objectives. If students do not follow the information, teachers must reteach, review, and reinforce the lesson and constantly convey higher expectations for learning the information. Consistent use and reinforcement of the CMP sends a strong and clear message that this is how the class works.

Introduce the CMP Early

Teachers need to introduce the CMP to students the first day of class for this is the time students must begin to understand the way teachers plan to work and how they plan to have the classroom work. Teachers can teach the need for and importance of a CMP with Sample Lesson 1 and also use this lesson plan to create, develop, and even review one or more components of the CMP.

CMP Mini-Lesson for Introducing the CMP and its Components

Grade Level: 1–12
Time: 10–30 minutes

Objectives

Students can

- recognize the need for and importance of a CMP or a component of the CMP.
- develop a component or strategy for the CMP.
- apply the CMP and its components to several classroom situations.

Opener

Ask students if the following quotes sound familiar.

"I'm finished with my work; what do I do now?"

"What is the homework policy?"

"What happens if I'm sick?"

"How will you grade this?"

Discuss the phrase, "I love it when a plan comes together!" Focus on such terms as *plans*, *procedures*, and *policies*. Tell them this class will have a classroom management plan, or CMP. Together, the class will develop a CMP that structures how the class will work.

Instruction

Ask students to brainstorm about why a classroom plan is important to both the teacher and students. Place their ideas on the chalkboard or overhead. Define the CMP as a plan to structure a secure, organized, effective learning environment conducive to meeting the needs of students through the day, class, or course.

Explain to students briefly that a CMP is a plan with components. Discuss the role you want students to have in creating or developing the components. Explain, for example, that students can create a component of the CMP such as a problem-solving strategy. Ask students why problem-solving strategies are important, and ask them to name some classroom problems. What, for example, was the first problem mentioned in the opener? Place student suggestions on the board for "I'm finished with my work; what do I do now?" Place students into groups and have them write scenarios that require problem-solving strategies, then have them share their scenarios and create problem-solving strategies to solve these problems.

Variation 1

Place students into groups of four students and give them an index card on which is written a scenario of a problem. Each card has a different scenario; for example, one card may read "John has been out of school for four days. He has a lot of work to make up. How can John get his work done?"

What kind of homework makeup policy should the class have? How can the class support John in getting his work done? Have students brainstorm then share their scenarios and suggestions for the homework policy.

Variation 2

Use a specific component of the CMP to demonstrate how the CMP works and students' role in developing the CMP.

Explain that students can develop a component of the CMP such as the homework policy. Ask them what a homework policy should tell a student and why such a policy is important, why it must be equitable, and why it must be enforced consistently. Explain that when a policy is in place, students know what is expected of them and know the consequences when they do not complete the homework. Introduce the homework policy in the CMP, and ask students to further develop it. Discuss the policy with students, and have them copy the policy in their notebooks. For younger students, place the policy on the bulletin board or a poster. Also, give students a copy to be signed by both the student and a parent and kept in their notebooks.

Closure

Ask students why the CMP is important and why the problem-solving strategies or homework policy or CMP will help them.

Teaching Classroom Rules

One of the first components of the CMP teachers should cover is classroom rules. Research supports establishing classroom rules early in the school year and allowing students to help create them. Students follow the rules they have developed more readily than those rules the teacher imposes on them. In addition, rules the class has developed collectively can engender class cohesiveness, strengthen student comradery, and support positive peer relationships (see also Figure 5.3).

Because the class develops the rules, this area of the CMP will require modification. When teaching rules or responsibilities, teachers may want to start with a CMP mini-lesson on why rules are important and what rules would benefit the class. During this lesson, students discuss and select the rules for their classroom. Teachers can plan a lesson for each rule or combine two or more rules into one lesson. Remember in the teaching and learning of the CMP, the teacher and students must share their expectations. For example, the rule "Be respectful," can produce conflicting expectations among different populations. To a teacher, being respectful may mean staying in one's seat, doing what is asked the first time, or remaining quiet at all times. To students, being respectful may mean saying "please"

FIGURE 5.3

The Rule of Thumb . . . and Fingers

Use the hand rule as a technique to remember and model the steps of good rule-making. The fingers of an outstretched hand serve as a reminder that five rules are enough for a classroom.

1. Raising the thumb, state that the class develops rules together.
2. Keeping the thumb raised, add the index finger, and state that class rules must be brief, clear, and stated positively.
3. Raising the next finger, state that class rules are to be posted, and students must memorize them.
4. Add the fourth finger, stating that class rules must be taught.
5. Raising the final finger, state that class rules require a commitment from all students in the class that they will follow the rules (consensus, show of hands, contract, etc.).

and "thank you" or being helpful. Respect, to a student, may have no reference to staying in one's seat or not talking. Sharing these perspectives makes everyone more mindful of how to make a classroom work.

Sample CMP mini-lessons 2 and 3 are designed to help create and teach classroom rules.

SAMPLE LESSON 2

CMP Mini-Lesson for Developing Classroom Rules

Grade: K–3
Time: 15 minutes

Materials
Coaching accouterments such as a sweat suit and whistle

Objectives
Students can

- identify words associated with *coach*.
- develop rules for working as a class team.
- work together in cooperative learning groups while establishing rules.

Opener
Enter the room wearing a sweat suit and baseball hat, with a whistle draped around your neck, and ask students, "Who am I?"

Instruction

After letting students guess your role, make a word web on the board, placing the word *coach* in the middle of the web, and ask students to provide words related to *coach*. Have students write these words in their journals.

Guide students to select such words as *team, goals, coaching, players, uniforms, hats*. Ask if they see any similarities between a teacher and the coach of a team. List some similarities on the board. Next ask what similarities exist between them as students and members of a sports team. Again, list these similarities.

Once you feel students can see how the class is similar to a team, ask them to name some rules a team member on a basketball team must follow. A soccer team? List their answers on the board. Then give students the opportunity to identify one rule they think the class team would need to follow to win this year's trophy for Best Class. Place students in groups. If students sit at tables, tape a baseball sticker or small piece of paper with a computer-generated sports graphic on it to one chair. Or simply hand one student in each group a sticker or the graphic. The student with the sticker or graphic records the group's suggestion. Tell them they have five minutes to work. Monitor student understanding by asking students to repeat what you have asked them to do. Identify the group recorder, and ask that student to explain his or her role. Ask students how long they have to complete the assignment and how many rules they are to submit.

Tell them you will time the activity, and when they have one minute left, you will write that on the board. When time is up, you will ring a bell. Again, ask them how they will know when they have a minute left. And how will they know time is up? Finally, ask if they have any questions before they begin.

After sounding the time's-up bell, call on the recorders to report to the class their group's rule. Write these rules on the board or overhead projector. As a class, talk about the rules and select, by means of a democratic vote, the first rule in making the class team successful.

Closure

Ask why the first rule is an important one. Have students copy the rule into their journals, and write the rule on the rule board.

SAMPLE LESSON 3

CMP Mini-Lesson for Teaching Classroom Rules: Respect

Grade: 4–8
Time: 15 minutes

Materials

Recording of Aretha Franklin's "RESPECT"

Objectives

Students can

- identify and define respect.
- explain three ways to show respect in the classroom.

Opener

Play a recording of Aretha Franklin's "RESPECT." Point to each letter of the word on the rules poster as Aretha sings it. Ask if the song gives them any hints about the topic of today's lesson.

Instruction

Tell students the class will create a working definition of respect for the class. Ask them what they think respect means, and place their answers in a web on the board. When they feel they have covered all of the major points, have them pair up with the person seated beside them for a think-pair-share activity. Tell them to decide on the most essential terms to describe or define respect and to be prepared to share their answer with the class in three minutes.

Ask for volunteers to share their group's ideas about the essential ingredients of respect. Write the terms on the board. Give students one minute to choose the term that is most important and then the term that is second in importance to include in the definition. Number each term as students choose it, first choice, second choice, and so on.

Let students formulate the class definition, then have students copy the definition into their journals or notebooks.

Now that the class has a definition of respect, ask them to consider another aspect of respect. Think about who and what deserves respect. Have them list their answers in their journal. Circulate among students and give positive feedback.

Have all students stand up. Tell them to remain standing as long as they have at least two items on their list. Then only those students with at least three items on their list stay standing. Then whose with five items on their list, then six, then eight, narrowing the field to the one or two students with the most statements on their list. Have those students list their items on the board.

Point out that many people, objects, and situations deserve respect. Ask if any student has an item not listed on the board, and, if so, add it to the list on the board. Have them copy the list into their journal. Go down the list and discuss how one should show respect to these people or in these circumstances or situations.

Closure

Ask for a volunteer to state the class definition of respect. Point to the first objective of the lesson on the board: students can identify and define respect. Ask students to name one way everyone can show respect in the classroom. Point to the second objective on the board: say that now the class knows at least three ways to show respect in the classroom. Why is this important?

Independent Practice
Have students write a paragraph explaining why respect is important in school and out of school.

Teaching Consequences

Place consequences in hierarchal order of severity. Begin with a nonverbal warning such as eye contact, proximity, or both. This first level is necessary because it serves as a reminder, doesn't stop instruction, and makes students accountable for their actions.

The second level in the hierarchy is expressing a clear verbal warning such as stating the inappropriate behavior and supplying an appropriate one, or using an I-statement. An I-statement expresses one's thoughts and feelings about another's actions or words. An I-statement conveys three points to students: 1) the inappropriate behavior; 2) how the teacher feels about the behavior; and 3) why the behavior is causing a problem (Charles 1999). In making an I-statement, follow this outline: I feel [tell the feeling] when you [say the reason] because [state the effect]; for example, "I feel frustrated when everyone talks at once because I can't hear what anyone is saying. Please raise your hand."

The class can choose a word, phrase, or cue that means, "Stop the inappropriate behavior now before it escalates beyond control." Examples of some words include "Freeze," meaning stop the behavior now; "Trouble in Paradise," meaning a problem exists; and "TLC," meaning everyone needs to offer **T**otal **L**earning **C**onsideration. Some cues include referee's signals and sign language. At this point, the student has one more opportunity to choose more appropriate behavior.

The next level is a cooling off period, sometimes called a time-out. This period provides students an opportunity to collect themselves by going to a planned place in the room or another room for a specified amount of time. Instead of a time-out, the teacher may want to schedule a conference at this level, which could involve a phone call to the parent. A student who gets to the third level needs a conference with the teacher to discuss how the student could avoid reaching this level in the future.

The fourth level may be a demerit, conduct notice, in-school suspension, or similar consequence. The final level may be a visit with the principal. Teachers can create their own hierarchy of consequences alone or solicit student input. If a student presents such problems as hitting or swearing, the student does not progress through the hierarchy but goes directly to the final level in the hierarchy.

Teach the consequences and the hierarchy to students. Get a commitment that they understand and agree with the consequences just as they gave a commitment to the rules. Whenever students have input into the components of the CMP, the teacher must include in the CMP mini-lesson the call for consensus and a show of commitment.

Discuss both the CMP and the consequence hierarchy with the principal in the beginning of the year. A principal can be an effective part of the CMP when he or she knows when the principal will be called into the plan. The lesson plan below can assist teachers in teaching consequences.

SAMPLE LESSON 4

CMP Mini-Lesson for Teaching Consequences

Grade: 2–6
Time: 20 minutes

Materials
Class rules poster, consequence list

Objectives
Students can

- understand consequences exist when they break the rules.

- explain the escalating consequences for continually breaking the rules.

Opener
With the poster of Class Rules in a prominent position, ask the class which of the class rules they think is most important. Write their answers on the board. Then take a vote. Say, for example, the class agrees that "Respect" is the most important rule to make the classroom a place where all can learn and work together. Have students list all the reasons respect is vital in the classroom. Tell them the class will discuss what happens when that rule, or any one of the other class rules, is broken.

Instruction
Discuss how someone who is not following the Respect rule might be behaving. Perhaps this person is talking and interrupting the teacher or making it difficult for fellow students to hear or to work. Ask students what the class should do in that situation. Should the class let the behavior continue? Should something be done to the rule-breaker? Should the student be chastised by the teacher? Sent to the principal? Be suspended?

Have students work in pairs to decide what should be done to the rule-breaker. Have students share their answers with the class, and list them on the board.

Discuss whether a student who has broken the rule only once should have to suffer the same consequences as someone who has broken the rule many times or broken many rules.

Post the hierarchy of consequences for rule infractions and discuss the levels. Read the list and demonstrate some of the consequences; for example, the first time you notice a student disrupting the class, you give a *nonverbal* warning. An example of a nonverbal warning is eye contact with the student. If the student doesn't cooperate after the first warning, he or she gets another chance to follow the rule.

Next, move very near a student and ask the class to describe the action. Ask if they think standing right on top of the student's desk will help quiet the rule-breaker. What should happen if the rule-breaker stops the behavior after either "The Look" or the "Close-Up"? Listen to class suggestions, then say that anyone who takes the hint and stops talking or disrupting the class after a nonverbal warning will be fine. If the behavior doesn't, the next step is necessary. Ask students to explain why the next step is necessary.

Explain that the next step is a *verbal* warning. If the chatty classmate does not take the nonverbal hints, you might say something like, "I feel disappointed when you talk when I'm giving instructions, Joe, because you are making it hard for the people around you to concentrate on what we're trying to learn." If mythical Joe Student stops talking and settles down for the rest of the day, nothing more will happen. Ask the class if the rule-breaker should suffer a consequence if he continues to cause problems. Point to the next step on the hierarchy of consequences.

For younger grades: the rule-breaker must move his car from green to amber on the class Behavior Stoplight, meaning the student has a warning. The next time the rule-breaker talks while the teacher is giving instruction, he has to move his car from amber to red. If the student is told to move to the red light, the student knows this behavior is unacceptable and must change immediately. The student moves the car and places a check by his or her name on the traffic control poster. One check means the student moves to the time-out chair for five minutes, the student signs the traffic ticket book, and a teacher-student conference is scheduled; two checks means a note home, and three an immediate call home.

For older students: the next step may be *The Note*. Joe Student goes to a time-out place and completes a note. In the note, Joe must explain how he broke the classroom rule and what he could do differently next time and pledge to try to behave more appropriately. The Note documents the behavior. If the student must complete a second note, both notes are sent home with a note from the teacher explaining the situation, asking for the parents' support in correcting the child's behavior, and requesting the parents' signature. Show students The Note and say, "This is what The Note looks like. I'm showing it to you now because I'm sure most of you will never have an opportunity to see one up close, RIGHT?"

Ask if everyone feels this is fair treatment. Get class consensus. If a student feels some unfairness, the student must explain why and suggest another way. The class discusses the new option and either agrees with the student or agrees to what had been suggested earlier.

Explain that the final step is a visit to the principal. Express the wish that they avoid that step.

Closure

Ask students to describe what happens the first time someone does not honor the respect rule. And if he or she doesn't take the nonverbal hint? What might the rule-breaker hear if the activity continues? If the behavior still doesn't stop, what happens? How can writing The Note help a student? What is the last resort?

Teaching Incentives

Spend time thinking about incentives. Incentives are inducements from teachers to students, ranging from simple incentives such as high fives, winks, thumbs up, and talk time to more elaborate gestures, opportunities, and experiences such as homework passes, Freedom Friday, field trips, guest speakers, and sign language instruction.

The incentives portion of the CMP needs student input, so this area will change somewhat based on that input. It is important to note that incentives, like rules and consequences, need a classroom show of agreement and commitment—a show of hands, contract, or other pact. All members of the class then work toward earning the agreed-upon incentives. Given this role in how the class operates, the class, then, becomes the students' class, not the teacher's class. This sense of student control, power, and autonomy supports how a classroom works and how teachers and students work in a classroom (see Figure 5.4).

FIGURE 5.4

The Teacher Who always Wore Pants

In one classroom, the class-selected incentive pertained to collecting compliments. Students decided that if the class received ten compliments, the teacher would perform one cartwheel. Students decided the more compliments, the more cartwheels. The compliments came from school staff, teachers, and parents. Students all worked together to be good to see the teacher do cartwheels. The teacher earned the reputation as the Cartwheel Teacher, and kids couldn't wait to get into her class so as to be good and earn compliments.

Remember, the goal is for students to choose the incentives readily over the consequences, to buy into the CMP instead of ignoring or rebelling against it. Thus, the incentives need to reflect student ownership, autonomy, and empowerment. The following CMP mini-lesson plan is one example of teaching classroom incentives to students.

CMP Mini-Lesson for Teaching Incentives

Grade: 1–8
Time: 15–20 minutes

Materials
Jar, marbles

Objectives
Students can

- identify appropriate behaviors that can earn marbles.
- recognize the cue for getting their attention.
- apply the marble jar incentive to classroom management and learning.

Opener
Hold up a jar. Hold up a package of marbles. Explain that Jar + Marbles = Incentive. Ask students what incentives are and why they are important. Ask them to guess how this jar will work in this classroom. Explain that the marble jar will collect earned "recognitions" and when it's filled, the class receives a recognition for a job well done (adapted from Canter and Canter 1976).

Instruction
Discuss how individual students and the class can earn marbles. When students or the class behave well, a marble or two goes into the jar. Ask students what behaviors might be worth a marble or two. Have the class make a list and copy the list into their notebooks, or place students into groups of two or more, and have each group identify five appropriate behaviors. Record the behaviors on the board.

Share specific examples of how students and the class can earn marbles. Discuss how they can help each other earn marbles. The following specific examples apply to grades 4–8.

- Exhibiting good behavior in the halls and to and from special events
- Displaying good citizenship
- Working diligently and productively on assignments
- Demonstrating good behavior in assemblies and other events outside of class
- Receiving compliments from others
- Honoring the class rules
- Following directions, routines, and procedures correctly
- Solving problems and making good choices

Place a few marbles in the jar and shake the jar, making a sound everyone can hear. Explain that when students hear this sound, they should stop all work and give full attention to the teacher. The marble jar also serves as a cue for getting students' attention.

Have students decide (vote) on the reward when the jar is filled. This marble jar incentive supports the entire CMP.

Closure
Ask students to explain how the marble jar works in this classroom. If they speak out of turn or do not raise their hands, shake the marble jar and see if they respond to the cue. Drop their first earned marble in the jar.

Teaching Social Skills

Many communities expect schools to focus more attention on developing social and cooperative student behaviors. Sylwester reminds educators how important it is to help students learn skills of cooperation. He states, "In our multicultural society, the school is the place where children from diverse backgrounds come together, and thus it is the best place for them to learn to work well with others" (1995, 118). If students pick on one another, say cruel things, complain, whine, and tattle, teachers should plan mini-lessons in developing more appropriate social behavior, strengthening interpersonal skills, and stressing the three Cs: cooperation, consideration, and civility. Sample CMP mini-lessons 6 and 7 have been developed to teach social skills.

SAMPLE LESSON 6

CMP Mini-Lesson for Teaching Social Skills: Friendship and Respect

Grade: K–3
Time: 30 minutes

Materials
The Giving Tree; (per student) 5" x 8" sheet of white unlined paper; 9" x 12" sheet of colored construction paper; 10 4-inch squares of brown tissue paper; 10 4-inch squares of light blue tissue paper; 20 squares of green tissue paper; paintbrush; half-glue and half-water mixture; glue; scissors; and pencil, crayons, or markers

Objectives
Students can

- define friendship and how it works.

- describe ways to make and keep friends.

Opener

Before this lesson, send a note home explaining the lesson and asking that each child bring in a small object they can give to a friend such as a drawing, painting, leaves, or something they baked.

Read *The Giving Tree* by Shel Silverstein to give students an understanding of the word *giving*. Ask every student how they feel when someone gives them a present.

Instruction

Start with a semantic web of student definitions of friendship, and discuss the book *The Giving Tree*.

Discuss different actions and situations in which people make friends and keep them. Have students get into their think-pair-share groups and come up with three acts of friendship.

Introduce friendship cards and explain using squares of colored tissue paper to form pictures. Explain that this is called a mosaic. Show examples of mosaics in an art book or a teacher-made example. Have students work in groups of four to make their own cards.

To make Friendship Cards, brush a mixture of half glue and half water on the center of the white paper. Place brown tissue paper on the wet area, overlapping the squares to make a tree trunk. Continue adding the glue-water mixture and tissue squares to make a tree scene with leaves (green), grass (green), and sky (blue). Brush the entire picture with the glue-water mixture. Let the picture dry. Trim the tissue squares from the edges of the white paper as needed. Fold construction paper in half to make a card. Glue the tissue paper picture to the front of the card.

Let students write a special message in the card for a friend.

Closure

Review each item the tree gives to the boy in the story. Have each child think of something he or she could do to make a friend happy. Have every student draw another student's name out of a box, and give the special object they brought to that person. Ask students what they learned.

Independent Practice

Have students write in their journals about their very best friend. Have them describe what a friend is, why they like their friend, and what they do for their friend.

CMP Mini-Lesson for Teaching Social Skills: Class Meetings

Grade: 3–8
Time: 10–15 minutes

Materials

Audiotape of stock market traders, T-chart with "Class Meeting Behaviors" printed at the top

Objectives

Students can

- identify both proper and improper class meeting behaviors.
- write four class meeting rules.

Opener

Play a 30-second excerpt of a tape of the stock market during trading time, with all of its seeming confusion. Ask students to take a minute to write down words that describe the scene. Make a T-chart labeled "Class Meeting Behaviors," with one side of the T-chart labeled Proper Behaviors and the other side, Improper Behaviors. Place the student responses under Improper Behaviors.

Discuss what a class meeting means to a classroom.

Instruction

Ask students to discuss why the behaviors listed on the board are not appropriate or conducive to a successful class meeting. Ask students to take a minute to think about the kinds of behaviors that are necessary for good class meetings. Have students pair up with their neighbor and for two minutes compile a list of proper behaviors for class meetings. Ask the pairs to share the behaviors. Write them on the T-chart, and have students copy them into their notebook. Have students form groups—two sets of pairs—and begin devising four class meeting rules. Have the groups share their ideas, discuss them, choose four, and vote on the rules. Place the rules for class meetings on a poster.

Closure

Ask how these behaviors help conduct business at a class meeting. Discuss what a teacher can do to support these rules and what students can do to support them.

Teaching Cues

Cues engender a response from students faster than words. Students often view teachers as talking too much, with students required to listen to every word. Nonverbal cues are quick, fun, and effective, and students like to figure them out by themselves without being told what to do.

It is essential to develop one cue to get everyone's attention. Another important cue is one that places students into pre-arranged group quickly and without discussion. An example of a cue for group work is to raise the index finger, which means students will work in their assigned think-pair-share partner arrangement. Raising the index finger and the next finger together means work with your table or row, whichever is appropriate. Raising four fingers means students should work in the group they are assigned to this month, and the extended hand means students should work in their own pre-selected groups of four students.

Sample mini-lessons 8 and 9 focus on teaching cues to the class.

SAMPLE LESSON 8

CMP Mini-Lesson for Teaching Cues

Grade: K–3
Time: 20 minutes

Objective
Students can

 • recognize the classroom cue and apply the five actions needed to follow it.

Opener
Draw a giant-sized hand on the chalkboard. Ask students what it might mean if you walk to the front of the room holding your hand in the air.

Instruction
Explain to students that your hand is the class cue, and you will use it to get the entire class' attention immediately, then they will follow five simple directions. Have students hold their hands up in the air while you explain the five steps they must take when you say, "Give me five!"

As you state each action, hold up one finger for each direction. The five actions are 1) Eyes on Me, 2) Mouths Quiet, 3) Bodies Still, 4) Hands Closed, and 5) Listen to Me (adapted from Wong and Wong, 1998).

Give students sample scenarios; for example, say "If I'm listening, sitting still, being quiet with my hands to myself, am I following the cue? Did I leave something out?" They should respond, "You forgot eyes on you!" While you teach this cue, randomly say "Give me five!" Check how many students are listening and following the cue. Each time you say the cue, review the five steps with students: Am I looking at the teacher? Is my mouth quiet? Is my body still? Are my hands closed? Am I listening?

Students enjoy repeating these phrases many times, and they will learn the five steps through repetition.

Closure

Have students repeat the five actions and write them on the board in each of the fingers. Have students continue to practice this cue. Eventually, students will keep themselves and their peers accountable for this cue each time they hear or see it.

Independent Practice

Have students trace their hands and label the fingers with the directions.

CMP Mini-Lesson for Teaching Cues

Grade: 4 and 5
Time: 15 minutes

Materials

Graduation gown, gavel

Objectives

Students can

- understand the purpose of a classroom cue.
- devise a classroom cue.

Opener

Dress in a black graduation gown and hold a gavel. Ask, "Who am I?"and "What's this?" Provide a short clip from the television program "Judge Judy."

Instruction

Ask students to describe what a judge does. Why does a judge need a gavel? Write student responses on the board. Ask students if order in the courtroom is important. If so, why? Ask them if order is also important in the classroom, and why.

Ask the class, if a judge uses a gavel to get attention and order in the courtroom, what should a teacher use in the classroom to get attention and order? Have students come up with the best "gavel" for the classroom, such as a whistle, bell, or clap sequence, then call their choice a cue. List their cue ideas on the board, and vote for the best cue. Ask when you should use the cue. Write their responses on the board. Tell students that for order and safety, it is imperative that the cue works. Ask them to raise their right hand and repeat the following: "I promise to uphold the cue of our classroom with the utmost respect and honor by following its purpose."

Closure

Ask students why it is important for a class to have a cue. Have them describe the class cue.

Teaching with a Computer

In addition to arranging desks, establishing reading corners, and preparing learning centers, today's teachers must plan computer areas. As the ratio of students to computers may be at best 25:2 in a classroom, it takes a commitment to technology and advance planning by the teacher to use computers in teaching and learning of lessons. Student use of computers, like learning centers, must reflect scheduled assigned groups. Teachers might, for example, schedule groups of students to work on computers by the days of the week as shown in the following chart (Figure 5.5).

FIGURE 5.5

	Mon.	**Tues.**	**Wed.**	**Thurs.**	**Fri.**
Group 1	Computer	Read text	Worksheet	Teacher	Project
Group 2	Teacher	Read text	Computer	Worksheet	Project
Group 3	Read text	Teacher	Worksheet	Computer	Project
Group 4	Read text	Computer	Teacher	Worksheet	Project
Group 5	Read text	Worksheet	Project	Teacher	Computer

SAMPLE LESSON 10

CMP Mini-Lesson for Teaching with a Computer

Grade: 1–5
Time: 20 minutes

Materials
Bow-tie pasta (one for each student), clear plastic container

Objectives
Students can

- review the computer programs available on the classroom computer.
- develop autonomy while taking turns on the computer.

Opener
Give each student one piece of bow-tie pasta. Have students write their student number on the noodle. (The number can be teacher-assigned or their number in the grade book.) Have them decorate their noodle around the number, then put the pasta into a clear plastic container.

Instruction
Ask students why people use computers and why they are so important. Make a semantic web of their responses, and have students copy the web. Explain to

students that the classroom has a computer center for them to use every morning. Provide an overview of the classroom's software programs.

To determine who will use the computer at certain times, place the container holding the pasta on the computer table. Explain that during computer center time, you will choose two pieces of pasta, and the two students with the numbers chosen will use the computers for 20 minutes. Explain you will continue choosing two pieces of pasta throughout the morning of each day to ensure all students have time at the computer. Plan for six students a day to use the computer center. At that rate, it takes a week to provide computer center time for all students in the class. Use a timer to keep track of the time.

Closure

Ask students to explain the procedure for computer use and copy it in their journals.

Independent Practice

Have students continue to follow this system of taking turns on the computer throughout the year. After a day or two, make students responsible for picking the pasta. This schedule enables them to work independently because they know what to do.

Chapter 6

Reflecting On and Revising the CMP

Every evening when she got home from school, Joan took her two dogs, Max and Spencer, for a walk. They walked along the creek near Johnson's farm, and while the boys romped and chased squirrels, Joan took advantage of the fresh air, the pastoral setting, and the time alone to reflect on her classes that day. She replayed the day in her mind's eye, thinking about what had gone wrong and what had gone right. On this particular day, she thought about a student who was struggling. When the dogs were tired from their play, they sat next to her on the grass under their favorite old tree, and she stroked them and wondered how she could help Stephen, who spent most of the time when he should have been writing in his journal doodling in its margins. He had a talent for drawing, that was clear, but how could she help him put that talent to use in her English class? By the time the dogs had gotten restless and were ready to head for home and their dinner bowls, she had devised a plan for him to draw a cartoon strip for the next writing assignment. When she reached home, she felt refreshed and invigorated. She took a few minutes to jot down ideas for the next day's lessons and wrote herself a note to talk with Stephen tomorrow. Her head clear, she headed to the kitchen for dinner.

A Plan in Flux

A dynamic plan, the CMP thrives on reflection and revision. Changing and improving the CMP provides an opportunity for professional growth and development. It is not a plan teachers can carve in stone and display in the classroom for all to read and memorize. Rather, it is more like clay teachers mold to suit their experience and their students.

The final phase of the classroom management process is reflecting on and revising the CMP. Reflection provides the impetus to change—it can be the vision teachers need to modify, revise, and try again. Teachers must reflect and revise on a routine basis. A Chesapeake, Virginia, teacher of the year, Lindsay Crump Porzio writes:

> Each year, I reflect on the following story and I renew my commitment to each and every student in my class:
>
> A retiring builder was asked to build one last house. Anxious to finish quickly, the builder used cheap materials and poor workmanship. When he finished, his employer handed him the keys and said, "Congratulations! This is your new house." The builder was shocked that he was to live in the poorly built house. If only he had built it better.
>
> As teachers we are the builders of the future and our "houses" are the young minds and spirits of children. Always we must use the best materials and organize our lessons with quality teaching moments. Every day we must ask ourselves, "Could I have done this better?" When we are handed the "keys," our reaction should be satisfaction. The future we build will be ours.

Teachers must continue to expand and develop their CMP. Not every choice and decision and action teachers make will work. And that's OK. Teachers learn with each success as well as with each failure, and they continue to improve their techniques. At the same time, they improve their methods for refining and implementing their plan. A teacher never needs to start a CMP from scratch again—just modify, improve, and continually strengthen it. This improvement is not only on paper but is in the teacher.

Reflective Revising of the CMP

Reflection and revising are important parts of the practice of teaching. To be and remain effective, teachers need to assess their own as well as students' classroom performance and behavior, analyzing and evaluating how they work and how the classroom works. Reflecting is a critique of a teaching lesson, learning activity, classroom situation, or behavioral problem. The evaluative aspects of reflection provide teachers with an opportunity to get in touch with their teaching selves, analyze their teaching goals, and chart a new course of action in achieving their goals. Kohn suggests that teachers be ". . . encouraged to think about their long-term goals and about whether their classrooms are really animated by these goals" (1996, 68).

This chapter guides teachers in reflection and CMP revising, instructing them how to take the time to reflect on the connection between what is going on in the classroom and the contents of the CMP. Teachers must train themselves to concentrate on and critique their teaching, student learning, and classroom management. A teacher can recall lessons, situations, problems, or concerns from memory, from notes taken during observations, and from videotapes of lessons and activities.

Students can also help teachers observe and reflect. Teachers should take the time to find out what students like and what they think works. Ask them which units they found most interesting and which were least interesting. Have them respond to a questionnaire with content such as "I feel good when Mr. Smith _____," or "I feel bad when _____ happens in class." At the end of the term or year, give them a list of the units covered during the period, and ask them to rank them according to which interested them most. Then ask them why they liked some units and not others. These methods of reflection in conjunction with a review of the CMP lead to constructive revising and refinement of the CMP.

Exploring Reflective Recall

The method designed for reflection and revising the CMP is called reflective recall. Reflective recall is a method that lets teachers use time, thought, and insight to impact how they and the classroom work. Reflective recall has a four-step approach: Stop, Recall, Review, and Revise.

In the first step, teachers must physically *stop* everything to spend time reflecting on a lesson, situation, problem, or concern. It is necessary for teachers to allot time routinely to stop the busy-ness of teaching and just think about their class, their teaching, and their students' learning. Teachers must also schedule a place to do this reflective thinking. Perhaps a place that is bright, a corner of a room with a window, a comfortable place. This place definitely needs to be out of the mainstream, away from phones and interruptions.

The next step is to *recall* lessons, events, situations, and experiences. Once stopped, teachers can begin to think about the day, morning or afternoon, or a unit of study, lesson, or objective or two, including their students' learning and everyone's effectiveness, willingness, and productivity. Teachers should focus solely on that recalled information.

In the *review* step, teachers think about the recalled information and connect it to the CMP. Teachers may want to reflect on this information alone or discuss the lesson, event, situation, or experience with a fellow teacher or friend. A good starting point is a reflection web with the situation, problem, or concern in the middle. Use the web to explore ways to change and improve the situation.

The following guidelines may help address the topic in the center of the reflection web.

• Review the CMP. It may simply be necessary to reteach a certain idea or strategy of the CMP.

• Add ideas or strategies to the CMP. With CMP in hand, look for more connections to students' control needs and ways to integrate the components of the CMP to address the situation.

• Review Glasser's student needs for belonging, power, fun, and freedom (see chapter 4), and attempt to provide more connections by including more opportunities, possibilities, and experiences in the CMP components to meet those student needs.

• Look for components or ideas that require strengthening or need more support to resolve the current situation. Once again, develop more support by integrating ideas in each component with ideas in other components.

The final step in reflective recall is to *revise*. Teachers can revise the CMP by adding, changing, or eliminating ideas or linking the components and ideas to each other. Teachers can develop the new components, ideas, and strategies with the class, then teach students the new CMP material. Once again, gain the commitment to the new input with student consensus. See also Figure 6.1.

Reflective Recall in Action

Seventh-grade teacher Lauren Peters sets aside time in her weekly schedule at school to reflect. She stops everything and, first, thinks about what is going well, then concentrates on a teaching or learning area that needs improvement. She recalls a problem pertaining to a cooperative learning activity. Lauren reflects on the situation and determines that her goal is to reduce the noise, decrease student movement in the room, and raise group productivity. Reviewing her CMP, she asks herself, "Do I have a rule that speaks to noise, being considerate of others, staying in your groups, or producing quality work?" If she doesn't, now would be the time to plan a CMP mini-lesson in which the class adds a new rule or two to support cooperative working situations. But Lauren does have such a rule: "Keep noise down to a considerate level."

Reflecting on her CMP and Glasser's identified student needs, she asks herself the following questions: Does the classroom meet each of these needs? Do my students need more direction, more specific procedures, or more appropriate assignments for group work? What components and ideas in my CMP could I strengthen or add to support this rule?

Next, Lauren thinks about what she can do to reduce the noise and foster more acceptable and productive work behavior. She ponders several options, including establishing a cue, developing rules for working relationships, or assigning roles in group work, in particular, a role for one student to monitor the noise level of the group.

She reviews the evaluation component of her CMP and decides she will add an incentive for students to demonstrate more effort and produce quality work. She double checks the group incentives component to ensure that such recognition exists. Then she plans a CMP mini-lesson for developing students' social skills that includes understanding the word *considerate* and getting class consensus on a definition and expectations for that word.

Lauren's final step in the reflective recall method is to revise her CMP to strengthen and maintain its efficient and effective operation in her classroom. She recognizes that a CMP must reflect the changing needs of the class and remain a dynamic plan for classroom management.

FIGURE 6.1

Reflecting through Videotape

Teachers can make a videotape of a lesson or activity and apply the same reflective recall method in working with the videotape.

- **Stop** the tape at different places.
- **Recall** what is happening.
- **Review** areas of the CMP pertaining to the situation on screen.
- **Revise** the CMP to strengthen weak areas.

As always, make plans to incorporate these new ideas into a CMP mini-lesson taught to students.

For Further Study

• Complete this statement in as many ways as you can. Reflective teachers are . . . .

• Take a lesson that didn't go well. Complete the reflection web by thinking of options for making the lesson work better. After completing the reflection web, review the CMP components and ideas, and revise the CMP.

Chapter 7

Samples of Effective Teachers' CMPs

When Bruce Gibson, an education major and preservice teacher, turned his CMP in to Professor Warburton, the professor found the following note attached to the plan.

"Dear Professor," it began. "I spent a lot of time on my CMP, and the more I thought about its content, the more I realized I had still more to think about, and the more I wrote, the more I realized the less I know about classroom management.

"So I turn this in because today is the due date, not because I am entirely satisfied with the product. Even as I placed it in your mailbox, I could see areas I wanted to revise. I guess what I'm saying is, as you review my plan, please understand that it is still a work in progress. I'm sure that by the time I step foot into my own classroom for the first time, I will have revised it, and by the time my first year of teaching is complete, it may, in fact, bear only a resemblance to the plan you now hold."

Professor Warburton smiled. He couldn't have asked for anything more. Bruce was going to be all right.

On Solid Ground with a CMP

No two CMPs are alike—each is unique to the teacher who composes it. According to Wong, the central difference between novice and experienced teachers is that successful teachers feel comfortable and in control of the teaching environment (1990). The classroom management process provides the beginning teacher with the foundation on which those feelings of competence and self-assurance form. For the practicing teacher, the classroom management process provides a guide to organize one's thoughts, behaviors, and practices into the CMP.

Ideas for a CMP are everywhere, and when they discover good ideas, good teachers add to and refine the CMP. The classroom management process makes it simple to structure classroom management into teaching and student learning and create a sense of community in the classroom. Teachers can replace the phrase "Some teachers have it and others do not" with "I can make classroom management happen!"

The following sample CMPs have been developed by both preservice teachers and practicing teachers. CMPs are included for all grade levels: primary (K–3), intermediate (4 and 5), middle (6–8), and secondary (9–12).

SAMPLE PLAN 1

My Personal Classroom Management Plan

Grade Level: *Primary*

Teaching Goal: *My job is to ensure that every child who comes through my classroom door feels he or she is special and knows that I care.*

CLASSROOM ORGANIZATION

Classroom Environment
Draw or describe room arrangement

> *The room is arranged so all students can easily see the chalkboard and Word Wall. The carpet area is used for whole group instruction, cooperative groups, and oral reading (Figure 7.1)*

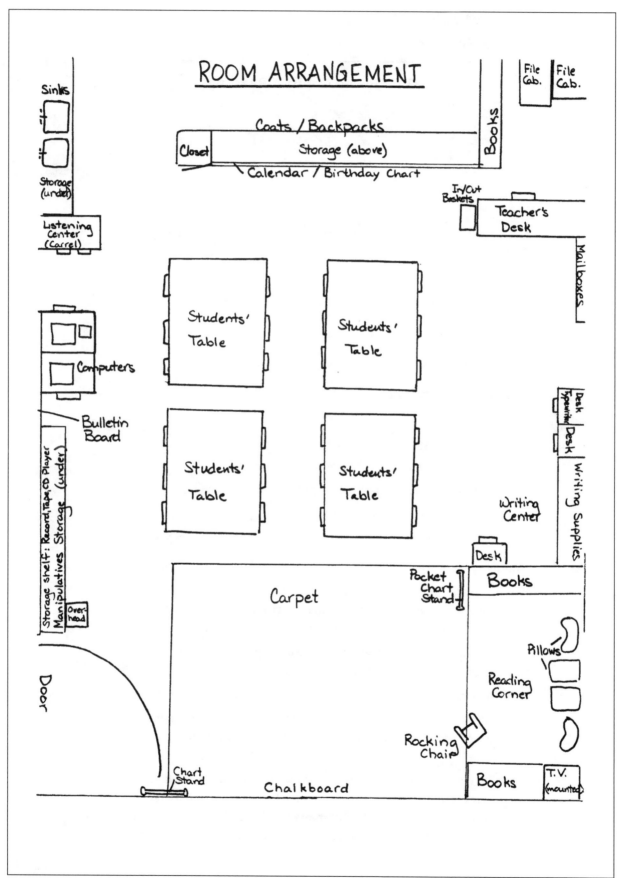

FIGURE 7.1
SkyLight Professional Development

Sketch bulletin board ideas

See Figure 7.2.

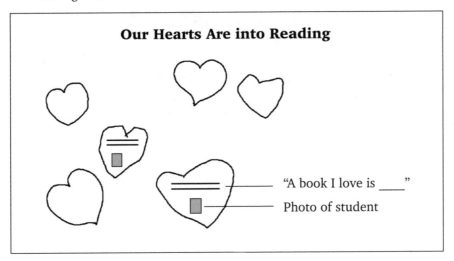

FIGURE 7.2

Class motto

The class motto is to treat others as you want to be treated.

Classroom Operation

Rules

Always be a good listener.

Raise your hand and wait to be called upon.

Keep your hands and feet to yourself.

Respect others and their belongings.

Follow directions.

Routines and procedures

Every morning, students organize themselves for the day, including bringing notes to me, unpacking books, and sharpening pencils. I write any important messages on the board for students to read in the morning.

Students put any homework into the appropriate homework tray and any notes from home into the teacher "in" box.

We write in our journals for fifteen minutes daily, teacher included.

After school announcements, I take attendance and lunch count. A student helper delivers the attendance card and lunch count to the appropriate place.

The class takes bathroom breaks according to the daily schedule, ideally, after lunch and before or after resource times. Students may get water at these times. For emergency bathroom breaks, students are instructed not to ask to leave during a lesson but may ask during independent work time.

Students sharpen two pencils in the morning. If their pencil breaks during the day, they set it in the "sharpen cup" on their desk, and one of the class helpers sharpens all these at an appropriate time.

Students are encouraged to complete work in a timely fashion. For students who finish early, various center activities are available to reinforce skills appropriate to the time. Students are also, on occasion, required to read silently or take accelerated reader (if applicable) tests. If the assignment allows for student helpers, students who finish early might be asked to assist those still working.

A Word Wall helps students with spelling. If a word is not found on the wall, students are encouraged to sound the word out or look it up in a dictionary.

In getting ready for lunch, students line up as follows: baggers buying nothing, baggers buying milk or dessert, those buying lunch according to their lunch choice, and according to rows/tables for popular lunch items.

I try to devote at least fifteen minutes three times weekly to math games during math time because children learn through play, and math games reinforce important skills in an entertaining manner.

All resource classes are observed, and I schedule in a daily recess time to give students a needed breather.

For the last few minutes of the day, I allow "talk time" with the radio playing quietly if students earn this through positive behavior.

Students must follow rules when working in cooperative groups. I teach "Rules for Working Together" along with cues such as "Give me five" and others to get students' attention.

The class holds weekly class meetings; a clipboard is posted for students to write questions and problems.

Students have stop signs on sticks, which they place in their sharpen can on their desk when they need teacher assistance during silent work time or tests. They work silently until I can get to them.

At the end of the day, students get time to pack up at their desk, then they are called by sections to get their belongings from the coat rack.

Students are dismissed from their seats when called to go home. Students stack the chairs before leaving the room.

Consequences

Students are introduced to a behavior program at the beginning of the year in which they "change the cards" for inappropriate behaviors. Every day students start with a blue card. If they have to be spoken to for inappropriate behavior, the following occurs: first, a warning; second, change card to yellow; third, change card to red and write a "think paper" to go home to parents about their behavior (parents sign the card, and students return it); fourth, referral to the principal's office.

Any severe behavior problems are referred to the principal immediately.

Incentives

I drop marbles into a small jar when students exhibit good conduct.

During warm weather, students earn free time on Friday by earning letters that spell RECESS. Appropriate behavior as a class earns them a letter. If all letters are earned by Friday, free time is awarded.

For individual rewards, students try to be "caught being good." Behaviors that are rewarded include being on task, walking quietly in the halls, doing what is asked of them, and being kind to others. Students receive a slip of paper and put their name on it. At the end of the day, any slips received are deposited into a class treasure chest. At the end of the week, one name is drawn and that person chooses a special prize. Then all names are discarded, and an empty chest starts the next week.

Students also receive happy grams for good test scores, awesome behavior, or kind deeds done unto others. These are sent home with students for parents to see.

Students receive "Smarties" or "Tootsie Rolls" intermittently when "caught being good" to activate the positive ripple effect.

Other incentives are a popcorn party, ice cream social, free time, doughnut party, or lunch in the classroom.

Cues

To regain class attention I use the following cues:

The phrase "Stop, look, and listen." Students freeze.

The phrase "All eyes on me." Students stop what they are doing.

Hand raised silently in the air—refocus attention on me.

Positive ripple effect: "I like the way Joe has his book opened to the right page, notebook opened and pencil sharpened." Others try to do the same thing to get recognition.

Lights Out: students understand this signals an emergency announcement.

Hand signals for group arrangements

A rap

INSTRUCTION

Lessons

Instructional strategies

Students have opportunities for individual, pair, and group learning experiences.

Use portfolios to monitor success.

Through cooperative learning activities, students learn to assume responsibilities and work efficiently with others.

Use hands-on learning.

Use computer to review basic skills.

Allow students to discuss work with peers.

Use constant visual checks for understanding while teaching—ask a question and have students respond either with a "thumbs up" or down or sitting and standing to get a visual check of who understands the lesson.

Teach lessons that allow for active student participation.

Have good openers to lessons and closure.

Write objectives on the corner of the chalkboard.

Use videotapes, audiotapes, and computer.

Individualized instructional strategies

Provide feedback immediately after class takes a test.

Students have the opportunity to read to me on several occasions.

Create different assignments for alternative learners.

Issue contracts for learning.

Provide help sessions.

Schedule volunteers to assist students.

Hold flex groups for small group learning.

Provide enrichment activities.

Allow students to choose some work to add to their portfolio.

Use individual file folders for practice.

Questioning strategies

Ask divergent and convergent questions.

Use response time.

Allow students to say "pass or play" when answering questions.

Use calling sticks to call on students randomly.

Ask preview and predict questions.

Ask why and what if questions—higher-level questions.

Ask, "Does anyone want to add to this answer?"

Examples of questions

What is figurative language?

Cite some examples from Amelia Bedelia.

Can you put this definition in your own words?

What was the most important issue facing the Puritans? Why?

Compare and contrast these ideas.

What might it be like in 2050?

What is your opinion on this issue?

What do you think about this topic? Why?

Find the evidence in your textbook.

Responses to students
   When a student gives a correct answer

   "Excellent."

   "Good job."

   Give a smile and a thumbs up.

   Use praise words such as "Exactly!" and "Yes!"

   When a student gives a partially correct answer

   "What else can you tell me?"

   "You are on the right track."

   "Keep thinking and I will come back to you."

   "Close. Can anyone else help?"

   When a student gives an incorrect answer

   "Let me give you some more information."

   "Wait a minute. Think about this, and I will come back to you."

   "Keep listening, and let's see what you come up with."

Student self-evaluation opportunities

   Check homework with a partner.

   Use answer keys.

   Choose work to place in their portfolio.

   Use calculators.

   Have informal conferences with teacher.

Effective Teaching Practices

Building positive relationships
   Between teacher and students

   Before the school year begins, students receive invitation postcards from me. On the first day of school, I share a little about myself by bringing in some personal items that describe and show them the type of person I am. Students are invited to bring in something to share about themselves on the days that follow.

   Students complete an interest survey during the first weeks of school. I use these to learn the likes and dislikes of my students.

   When possible, I greet students at the door in the morning and say good-bye to them as they leave in the afternoon.

   Occasionally, students are invited to eat in the classroom for a lunch time social. This allows me to learn some of their interests.

Among classmates

Cooperative learning activities

Peer editing

Checking each other's work

Class jobs in pairs

Peer assisting and tutoring

Applause for each other

Show and tell

Homework buddies

Games

With parents

During the first week of school, I write a letter home to the parents to introduce myself, explain my class philosophy, and make them aware of my expectations of their children.

During the first month, I make phone calls to all parents.

At the beginning of a new unit, I send home a newsletter to parents to explain to them what we are studying.

I ask parents to send in anything they might have to enhance the unit or to come in to speak with the class.

I hold conferences with parents to discuss any concerns and achievements of students throughout the school year. These conferences might be initiated by me or the parents.

I send home weekly papers to inform parents of their child's progress. A behavior sheet for the week is attached to the papers, so parents are aware of good and bad behavior. These are signed and returned to ensure parents see them.

Strategies to develop student social skills

Conduct CMP mini-lessons to discuss appropriate and inappropriate behavior.

Students work with their classmates frequently to discuss ideas and complete assignments.

Provide opportunities for students to practice their best manners, such as Author Teas and Mother's Day/Father's Day luncheons.

Give good citizen badges to students.

Honor the Student of the Week.

Give "caught getting along" recognition.

Strategies to develop student problem-solving and decision-making skills

> *Have students work in pairs and small groups.*
>
> *Give hands-on activities.*
>
> *Allow students choices in projects.*
>
> *Ask three before me.*

Strategies to develop student self-control

> *Give praise for appropriate behavior.*
>
> *Discuss why it is important to follow directions and behave.*
>
> *Give behavior tickets.*
>
> *Use self-monitoring charts and checks.*

Preventive discipline strategies

> *Use eye contact and proximity.*
>
> *Use positive reinforcement to encourage the ripple effect.*
>
> *Use I-statements.*
>
> *Use token economy.*
>
> *Monitor and mentor throughout lessons, moving around the room as I teach.*
>
> *Use cues and signals.*
>
> *Post class rules in a prominent location.*
>
> *Practice "withitness."*
>
> *Monitor continually.*
>
> *Get to know students and what is going on in their lives.*

Classroom technology plan

> *Technology is an important part of my classroom. Whenever possible, students work on computers. Computer lab time helps students become familiar with the different components of the computer. I implement age-appropriate software, both for research and pleasure. I publish student work on the computer and use e-mail for class pen pal projects.*

ASSESSMENT

Grading Plan

> *Students undergo evaluation in language arts, math, spelling, writing, social studies, and science. The types of grades assigned depend on the policy of the school system. Quizzes and homework receive a grade. Tests count double. Participation is averaged into the final grade. When report cards are issued, I hold a conference with every student about their grades and progress.*

Recording grades in the grade book

I place grades in the grade book according to subject area. I record test grades in red and all others in black. I check off a row at the bottom of the grade book as I enter grades into the computer. Students are assigned a number for easier recording and filing purposes.

Homework policy

Students write homework in a composition book every day. It is the students' responsibility to bring their composition book to and from school every day. Unless certain circumstances arise, students have one assignment a day that takes approximately twenty to thirty minutes. I check homework the following day but do not grade it since assistance is usually given in the lower grades. Students who do not turn in homework in a timely fashion make it up in the classroom and make up missed homework during free time in the room. Students receive a weekly homework sheet with a list of assignments.

Progress reports

I issue progress reports in accordance with the city policy. Students and parents are able to assess progress through the weekly papers sent home.

Student opportunities to impact grades

Extra credit: *Yes, they have the opportunity to receive bonus points on tests or quizzes. Each subject has an extra credit folder that allows them to earn points toward their final grade.*

Rewrites: *No*

Drop a grade: *Possibly. I drop a grade only if the majority of the class does poorly, then review and retest.*

Special Assignments: *Yes*

Collection of points factored into final grade: *Yes, students receive points for cooperative learning activities and homework.*

REFLECTION

Reflection time is essential for teachers to collect their ideas on the day's events as well as plan for the days to come. On Thursdays, I eat lunch in my room and reflect on my teaching and the students' learning. I use the drive to and from school to reflect on my effectiveness at school. All teachers of my grade level stay at school each Monday after school to plan the week's lessons together.

My Personal Classroom Management Plan

Grade Level: *Intermediate*

Teaching Goal: *Every child deserves a caring, enthusiastic, knowledgeable teacher who makes learning exciting, challenging, and fun.*

CLASSROOM ORGANIZATION

Classroom Environment
Draw or describe room arrangement

> *See Figure 7.3*

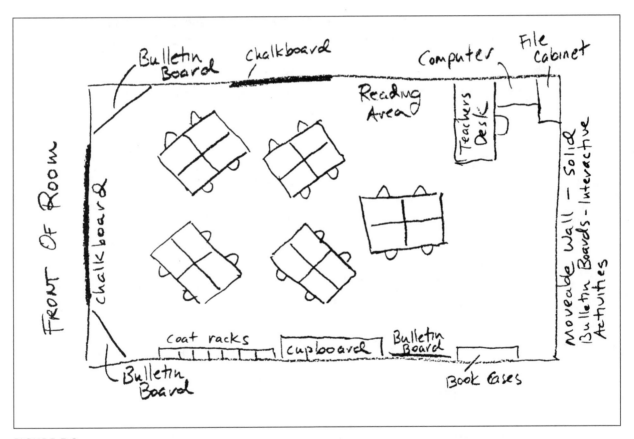

FIGURE 7.3

Sketch bulletin board ideas.

Students make daffodils out of construction and tissue paper, and write their name on the flower stem. We label the board "Learning Is in Bloom." The flowers also work well as a door decoration (Figure 7.4).

FIGURE 7.4

Class motto

(We say this each morning after the pledge of allegiance.)

I believe I can be a good student.

I believe I can achieve.

I believe that if I work hard, I will succeed.

Therefore, I will work hard each day to do my best.

I can learn.

I will learn! (Boyer 1995, 19)

Classroom Operation

Rules

Follow directions.

One person speaks at a time.

Mind your own business.

Keep feet, hands, objects to yourself.

Use encouraging words.

Routines and procedures

I greet students at the door with a handshake and a warm greeting, and sometimes the "helper" helps me greet them. Upon entering the classroom in the morning, students take their magnetic name strip off the blackboard and put it on a chart indicating their lunch choice, which helps do lunch count and attendance quickly. Students write in their journals every morning. A teacher read-aloud occurs daily right after lunch recess to calm students down and prepare them for the afternoon.

"Specials" are scheduled daily for one hour and include art, physical education, music, library, computer lab.

Music plays in the morning while students prepare for the day and also sometimes during free reading and writing times.

Two wooden bathroom passes are on hooks, and when needed, students take a pass and put it on their desk, use the restroom, and return quickly. They can't leave the room if I am doing directed teaching unless it is an emergency.

Students may sharpen pencils as needed except during directed teaching.

After the routine is firmly established, a student helper has a stamp pad and stamp and helps fill out the Bingo sheets by collecting homework and stamping.

Students have a plan book in which they write down each assignment. They copy homework assignments and highlight them. The plan book goes home daily, and parents are asked to look for highlighted areas. Parents sign the plan book on weekends, unless a student has a problem with responsibility, then the plan book gets signed nightly.

Students have a folder with inside pockets. One pocket is labeled HOMEWORK, the other GRADED PAPERS and INFORMATION. Students keep the folder on their desk all day, and organize handouts as they arrive. This folder goes home each night and is to be returned each morning.

Consequences

Nonverbal reminder

Verbal reminder

Time-out: 15 minutes in classroom; fill out think sheet for parent signature.

Time-out: 30 minutes in another classroom; fill out think sheet for parent signature.

Severe clause: referral to the principal's office.

Incentives

Verbal incentives

Positive notes

Phone calls

Extra privileges

Projects

Certificates

Recesses

Free reading

Happy face stamp on hand, notebook, or index card on desks

Computer time

Lunch with teacher

Sit at teacher's desk all day

Sit in teacher's chair

Teach a short lesson (supervised)

Individual incentives: Students begin each month with a Bingo sheet with 20 squares. They receive stamps for returning homework and notes or when "caught being good." When the sheet is filled, they draw out of a basket a cut-out on which is written an award, which is one of the incentives above. Students can fill more than one Bingo sheet each month.

Group incentives: Sometimes we do table points for rewards. Also, I use a time bank: I put minutes in a bank on the board when they cooperate and save minutes—30 minutes earns a recess.

On the wall in large letters is the word CATCHING. At the beginning of the school year I pass out letters that spell COMPLIMENTS. Students work in pairs decorating the letters (ownership). I laminate them and put them in a large envelope under the words CATCHING. When the whole class receives a compliment from another teacher, playground aides, or other staff, we post a letter until COMPLIMENTS is spelled out. Then we have a special class party, and start the process all over again.

Cues

Bell signal

Finger to the lips

Wink

Head shake

Frown

Smile

Snap fingers

Clap hands

Count down–5, 4, 3, 2, 1

INSTRUCTION

Lessons

Instructional strategies

Cooperative learning groups: One way I select cooperative groups is to distribute colored sticks, and students silently match colors to form new groups. I use a variety of ways to divide students into groups:

Pair-share

Team-pair-solo: Students read and do activity or problem as a whole group or team (teach new concept, for example), then divide into pairs and do further work on the activity or problem with more details. For the solo portion, they must answer the problem or question to show understanding of the concept.

Study guides

Journal writing: responses and explanations used in math, science, and social studies

Projects

Scoring guides

Alternate activities

Hands-on activities within lesson when possible

Thematic units

Skits and plays

Experiments, field trips, guest speakers, films, videos, or projects to strengthen skills or concepts taught

Create fun openers to lessons.

Focus students' attention on objectives of the lesson.

Give clear, step-by-step instructions, and always practice give-and-get in direction-giving.

Always close a lesson using questioning techniques relating back to the lesson objective(s).

Make learning fun and find purpose in all learning.

Individualized instructional strategies

In some cases, give students pretests, and if they receive 95 percent or higher, they may do alternate activities.

Let students choose some of their own spelling words.

Let students do "Invent your own homework." They choose their own activity to work on and share with the class.

Use activities—bulletin boards, centers, brain busters—that foster individualized learning.

Use the tic-tac-toe format. Different activities appear on a form (standard tic-tac-toe grid) at different levels of Bloom's Taxonomy after a theme or unit of study. Students sign a contract for what they will complete—two tic-tac-toe rows (diagonal, horizontal, vertical) for an A and so on. Students select activities.

Use portfolios and student assessments to build success.

Have students sign contracts whenever possible to hold them accountable for their learning.

Always be enthusiastic—give praise, positive comments, and handshakes, and smile often!

Questioning strategies

Just recalling knowledge

Comprehension questions

Probing and extending

Examples of questions

What is the author's purpose?

Give an example of fact and opinion statements.

Should Peter have acted the way he did when Fudge scribbled on his project?

Responses to students

When a student gives a correct answer

Validate the answer.

Don't repeat it; have another student repeat the answer and tell why it is correct.

When a student gives a partially correct answer

Use the information given and reword the question.

Turn to a partner and see if he or she can give rest of answer.

Let students talk it over and have the first student then give correct answer.

When a student gives an incorrect answer

Say "That's the answer to another question I was thinking of—way to go!"

"Now, listen again as I ask the original question," then reword the question.

"Talk to your Study Buddy and see if the two of you can figure out the answer."

"Listen to your friend answer the question, then I want you to repeat the answer."

Always dignify their answer, but hold them accountable.

Student self-evaluation opportunities

At the end of each project/presentation, students receive a form (tailored to each) on which they evaluate their effort, quality of work, and so on. I fill one out also, and we have a conference on the forms.

Students receive a blank report card (before I send it home), evaluate their work, and make comments.

They set goals each quarter, and write an evaluation at the end of the quarter (which goes into the report card envelope) stating whether they met their goal and explaining why or why not.

Students graph their progress on assignments, quizzes, and so on.

Effective Teaching Practices

Building positive relationships

Between teacher and students

Make announcements on the intercom about successes in the room.

Greet students at the door each morning either with a handshake or brief comments. At night I walk them to the bus and give them another handshake or pat and brief wishes for a good evening.

Eat lunch with students in the classroom and sometimes in the cafeteria.

Dialogue in journals; I comment on their entries, and ask and answer questions.

Give them notes, happy grams, stickers

Among classmates

Group work

Buddy system

Peer tutoring

Desk clusters

Group names

Catch them complimenting or encouraging each other.

With parents

Phone calls to parents about student successes

Weekly class-written newsletter

Notes in student plan books

Invitations to project presentations

Open-door policy in the classroom

Introductory letter

Strategies to develop student social skills

Our school has a program to develop social skills called Responsibility, Effort, Solving problems, Perseverance, Empathy, Cooperation, Teamwork (RESPECT). The skills are introduced on the intercom by groups of students through raps, poems, and other ways. Each teacher follows up in his or her own classroom by using literature, games, writing activities, and so on.

Fourth-graders and fifth-graders meet on a regular basis to do fun activities such as reading and writing.

Hold class meetings to build teamwork, plan activities, and solve conflicts.

Strategies to develop student problem-solving and decision-making skills

Students ALWAYS are problem solving from formal math to brain teasers.

Use interactive bulletin boards.

Solve class problems with class meetings.

Complete assessment tasks for new Missouri Assessment Project (MAP).

Use contracts: students decide what grades they want to make and decide upon activities, projects, presentations.

Use portfolios: students select which work goes into them and why.

Students earn and decide upon reward parties and do all the planning and organizing for them.

At times students choose which literature book and group they wish to work in. They decide who they want to sit next to at assemblies. I remind them of class expectations, then they choose.

Strategies to develop student self-control

Use the restroom when needed: two passes hang on magnets; students take a pass and put it on their desk, and when they return to the room, they hang the pass back up.

Sharpen pencils when needed.

Use any and all of teacher's supplies and manipulatives as needed.

Move around room as needed.

Select their own "Quality Papers" for portfolio.

Always give students choices.

Preventive discipline strategies

Nonverbals

Body language

Eye contact

Proximity

Touching on shoulder, head, hand.

Classroom technology plan

Students attend computer lab twice a week for thirty-minute periods. They use the Internet, Encarta, and various software.

ASSESSMENT

Grading Plan

Tests count twice. Projects, if assessment tasks, count as tests.

Recording grades in the grade book

I write the assignment title plus the percentage grade in the grade book. I draw a box around late and missing assignments and put in the grade when students complete the assignment. I can tell at a glance which students have poor study skills.

Homework policy

Our homework policy is a well-defined policy outlined in detail to students and parents at the beginning of the school year. It requires parents', students', and teacher's signatures. Briefly, five late assignments (ie, not ready by 8:45 a.m.) result in an after-school detention. After the detention, students start over with a clean slate. Each quarter, late assignments are erased and each student starts with zero demerits.

Progress reports

Progress reports are called "mid-quarters," and each student receives one halfway through the quarter. The form allows for percentage grades for each subject and comments and suggestions for remediation if necessary. This form requires a parental signature so "no surprises" occur at report card time.

Student opportunities to impact grades

Extra credit: *Yes*

Rewrites: *Yes*

Drop a grade: *No*

Special assignments: *Yes*

Collection of points to be factored into the final grade: *No*

REFLECTION

There seems to be no time during school. After school I often reflect on lessons that went well or didn't go as well as I expected. I make notes on the lesson plans or in the teacher's guide. I spend evenings on reflections and make changes in the next day's lesson plans. Approximately once a month our regularly scheduled faculty meeting is devoted to professional development. In addition, three daylong teacher inservice programs are scheduled per year.

My Personal Classroom Management Plan

Grade Level: *Middle*

Teaching Goal: *Leave the classroom better than I found it!*

CLASSROOM ORGANIZATION

Classroom Environment

Draw or describe room arrangement

> *My classroom looks like a traditional classroom for the first four or five weeks; however, after I start the cooperative learning groups the classroom changes. Seats are assigned by learning groups, as indicated by broken lines in Figure 7.5, and set up in a semicircle around the front of the room. Each of the four corners of the room fulfills an important role in helping me teach. One corner acts as a time-out center. The second corner is a reward type "living room" with easy chairs and rugs. The third is a computer center, and the last corner contains a large table and bookcase and functions as a book/reading/meeting place.*

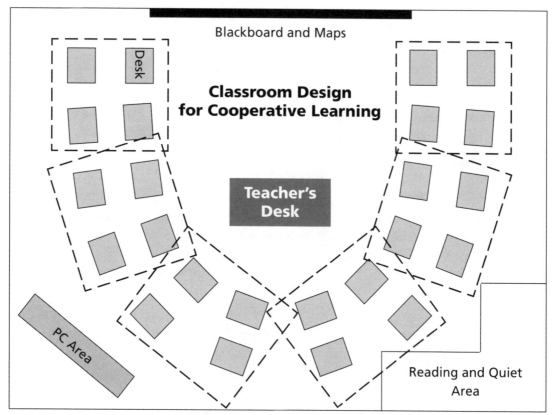

FIGURE 7.5

Sketch bulletin board ideas

The February "Famous Americans" unit highlights a person of the day. A picture of the person and a description strip are added to the board and discussed (see Figure 7.6).

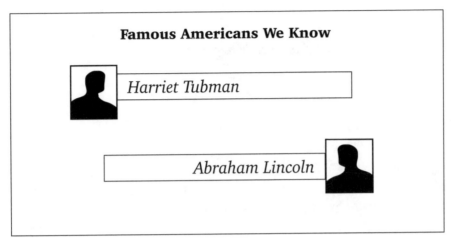

FIGURE 7.6

Class motto

We are all in this together!

Knowledge is power!

Classroom Operation

Rules

Be prepared.

Be respectful to everyone.

Be responsible.

Participate in class activities.

Obey all school rules.

Routines and procedures

Students are to sharpen pencils when they arrive in the classroom, before the bell rings. Once class starts, I cover the sharpener with an old sock. They then know not to approach the sharpener and not to ask to sharpen their pencil. For those who miss the chance, I have an "out" can with sharpened pencils they can borrow and an "in" can for unsharpened pencils.

All class work and homework assignments are numbered and posted in the classroom. Students who miss a day of school do not ask me what they missed; instead, they take responsibility and copy the missed assignments from the chart.

I or any student can call a class meeting to talk about rule violations or any other problem. The procedure is to place a note in the basket asking for a meeting the next day. The class meeting supports classroom participation and teaches problem solving.

Students section their three-ring notebook by subject. Each section has a table of contents listing assigned work, my letter to the parents stating my grading policy, and a parent review sheet. All assignments are numbered and returned to students for them to place them in the notebook in order. Parents can review the notebook any time and identify any missing assignments by means of the numbering. It is the student's responsibility to keep the notebook updated; however, I perform notebook checks routinely.

The class establishes cooperative learning rules, creates procedures, and shares expectations to aid the efficiency, effectiveness, and productivity of students when working in cooperative learning groups. I provide specific and simple directions either through handouts or by writing them on the chalkboard. I teach each step and ask students to summarize the directions. I establish cues that tell students to focus attention on me. I set a time limit for each step in the process, give the cue for students to enter their groups, then I circulate and monitor group progress.

Every week, I take the classroom climate, which tells me how students rate the learning environment of the past week. Students turn in a climate sheet without a name so they can comment without fear. They rate the environment on a scale of one to ten, with one being poor and ten, the best. They also tell me what they liked and disliked about the past week's instruction. Each Monday morning, after they turn in homework, we discuss the previous week's climate sheets. This routine gets students involved in the class, provides me with feedback, and allows me to point out behaviors that either help or hinder the class.

Tuesday through Friday morning routine is students turn in homework and write in journals for five to ten minutes on the most important lesson(s) they learned the day before, either in or out of school.

Each day has an ending routine; closure activities of the day include writing homework assignments, discussing the day's lessons and, if earned, free talk time.

Consequences (in order of implementation)
  Logical consequences:

   Those in which students must make right what they have done wrong

   If they make a mess, they clean it.

   If they willfully damage material, they must replace it.

  Generic consequences:

   Nonverbal cues including eye contact, proximity, body language/hand signal

   Verbal cues including use of student's name, I-statement, signal words, eg,

"Stop," "Check yourself," or words students select to signal inappropriate behavior

Conventional consequences:

Time out where student goes to assigned place either in or out of the classroom during student's free time (lunch time, time between classes, etc.)

Conference with student during student's free time

Written conduct notice or telephone conference with parent and/or school detention

In-school parent conference

Visit with principal

In-school suspension, suspension

Incentives

Group incentives:

"Talk time" during class time

Class parties

Freedom Fridays

Individual incentives:

Homework passes

Point coupons, worth points for graded assignments

Free time for library use and activities centers

Overtime reward certificate placed on the bulletin board when I "catch" a student putting in more than 100% effort

Cues

Counting backward from five

Raising a hand and moving to the front of the room

Turning the lights on and off

Crossing my arms and tapping my foot in front of the class

A whistle, bell, or chime

INSTRUCTION

Lessons

Instructional strategies

I believe an active classroom supports greater learning. My teaching strategy for the first four to five weeks of the school year is a traditional teaching manner, with enough activity to keep students from getting bored. This allows me to establish credibility as a teacher, teach the social skills and rules, and gather information on students' abilities.

After I have all the information I need and I have established myself, we move into cooperative learning groups. I feel the use of cooperative learning has many advantages over traditional methods, including greater use of higher-level reasoning, more on-task behavior, increased motivation, persistence in completing tasks, and better general attitudes toward school.

Enrichment of student learning is a powerful tool. Field trips, guest speakers, videotapes, and other resources provide students with a real, "live" look at where their education can take them and possible goals for their future.

Questioning strategies

> *Use higher-level questioning.*
>
> *Have students write questions instead of answers.*
>
> *Use Bloom's Taxonomy to formulate questions.*
>
> *Prompt, probe for answers.*
>
> *Use piggyback questioning.*
>
> *Ask "Why?"*

Examples of questions

> *Why do you think that happened?*
>
> *Persuade me to choose that product.*

Responses to students

When a student gives a correct answer

> *"Exactly!"*
>
> *"Absolutely."*
>
> *"You got that right!"*
>
> *"Yea!"*
>
> *Silent clap*
>
> *Thumbs up*

When a student gives a partially correct answer

> *"Keep going."*
>
> *"Add some more ideas."*
>
> *"Think about this; now tell me what you think."*

When a student gives an incorrect answer

> *"Whoa, slow down. Let's get some more facts!"*
>
> *"Let's discuss this more, then return to that question."*
>
> *"Scratch that for now!"*

Student self-evaluation opportunities

Check their own work.

Exchange papers.

Use the answer sheet.

Use portfolios.

Graph progress.

Keep a progress folder.

Perform self-evaluation inventories.

Effective Teaching Practices

Building positive relationships

Between teacher and student

Help sessions

Greeting students at the door

Class climate surveys

Agendas and schedules

Among classmates

Classroom buddy system

Information scavenger hunt about students

Interview other students and share the information

Student spotlight

Student mentoring and tutoring

Cooperative learning

Conflict resolution role-playing

With parents

Have parents act as guest speakers.

Class-written newsletters

Telephone calls

Notes

Strategies to develop social skills

Students design a name plate they feels represents them, then explain their design to the class.

A pair of students interviews and introduces each other to the class.

The class participates in a scavenger hunt to find out information about classmates such as who has a pet? Who likes baseball?

Teach and model good social skills.

Teach how to get into and work in groups, how to talk to each other, and how to display respect, and teach conflict management skills.

Observe groups as they perform activities and, specifically, look for evidence that students are practicing interpersonal/social skills. Give feedback and reinforcement to the groups using these skills.

Strategies to develop student problem-solving and decision-making skills

Improved problem-solving and decision-making abilities are two major benefits of cooperative learning. The ability to solve problems requires many of the social skills students must learn to be effective at establishing relationships and at collaborative learning. As a group, students must decide how to pursue whatever task they have been assigned or even pick the assignment themselves. I believe the motivation, persistence, and higher-level reasoning skills used in cooperative learning are the same as those used in decision making. By putting students into situations where they must use these skills, we teach decision making. In addition, I teach problem-solving and decision-making skills by means of CMP mini-lessons.

Strategies to develop student self-control

Conflict resolution strategies

Peer resolution

Peer mediating

Contracts

Preventive discipline strategies

Behavior modification involves the general use of positive and logical consequences to change student behavior. As a rule I do not use punishment, or negative reinforcers, because they prove less effective. The method I use involves identifying the behaviors that are to receive special attention and deciding which of the four positive reinforcers, social, graphic, activity, or tangible, to use.

First and foremost, I teach the class rules, incentives, and consequences. Other strategies include use of contracts between students and me and providing routines for the day-to-day operation of the classroom. My goal is to foster a sense of togetherness by regularly talking with the class about what they can accomplish as a group and teaching them how to deal with problems they encounter.

Classroom technology plan

My class uses computers. Software is acquired to supplement class learning. I also use videotapes, CDS, and the Internet. The computer lab is used for writing assignments and skills practice. The class corresponds with another middle school class in another state via e-mail.

ASSESSMENT

Grading Plan

I use the grading scale of the school system in which I teach. I believe students' time and effort are important to include in the grade. Because of this, every item of work students turn in has some point value, and the student receives feedback. This allows students to bring up their point level and shows them that everything they turn in is important to me and has value. Tests count double.

Recording grades in the grade book

Each student receives a number that coincides with their placement in the grade book. They write this number next to their name on all completed work.

Homework policy

Homework reinforces the day's lessons. My policy is to assign no more than an hour of homework Monday through Thursday, with no work on Fridays and weekends. The routine for turning in homework and other collectable work is as follows: each learning group has a manager. The manager collects the work from the group members and turns it over to the class manager who, with the help of the assistant manager, places the collected work in student number order.

Progress reports

Progress reports are issued as the school system requires.

Student opportunities to impact grades

Extra credit opportunities: I believe effort is important, and I provide opportunities for students to improve their grade by doing extra credit work. Also, students receive extra credit points for returning forms the next day and for bringing parents into the classroom as volunteers or for getting parents to attend Open House, conferences, and so on.

Rewrite opportunities: Students may rewrite some assignments, but the rewrite is averaged with the first grade to get a new grade. For example, a student writes a paper, receives a "C," and asks for a rewrite. The rewritten paper receives an "A." When the two grades are averaged, the paper receives a "B."

Drop a grade: When all homework has a point value and students are allowed to rewrite assignments, the need to drop grades does not come up.

Point system: Each question, or problem, in an assignment has a point value. The points are arranged on a continuum with a range of points assigned a letter grade. At predetermined times in the school marking period, I divide the total number of points the student earns, including extra credit, by the maximum total possible points, excluding the extra credit work to determine a percentage that corresponds with a letter grade on the continuum.

REFLECTION

Over the years I have found only two ways to improve at anything: First, ask those with more knowledge or skills to show me how it's done. I ask teachers who I feel have a complementary style to help teach me what I need to know. Second, I read every publication or book I can that contains useful information to take to the classroom.

Teaming in the middle school provides an extra planning bell that gives teachers time to meet together and plan lessons. We discuss certain students, situation, and problems. We reflect on our role in the students' success or failure.

SAMPLE PLAN 4

My Personal Classroom Management Plan

Grade Level: *Secondary*

Teaching Goal: *Make it relevant. Make it worth learning. Make it impossible to forget!*

CLASSROOM ORGANIZATION

Classroom Environment
Draw or describe room arrangement

My classroom has no teacher's desk. All desks face the room's center to generate an open forum of discussion, action, and sharing (see Figure 7.7).

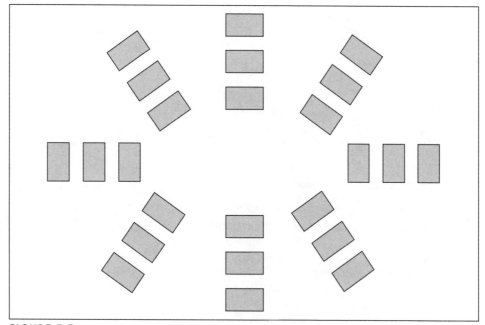

FIGURE 7.7

Sketch bulletin board ideas

See Figure 7.8. Under "Past," there might be a news story or other document pertaining to the 1960s civil rights movement. "Today" might highlight a current news story describing the continued struggle for human rights and racial harmony. Under "Tomorrow," I post student essays reflecting student opinions, insights, and solutions on the topic of human rights.

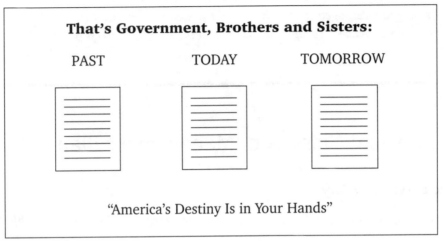

FIGURE 7.8

Class motto

What you lack is experience, not intelligence!

America's destiny is in your hands!

If you don't like it, work to make it better!

Equality is another word for mediocrity. Strive to be the best, better than the rest!

Classroom Operation

Rules

Respect yourself.

Respect others.

Respect this class.

Routines and procedures

Political cartoon for discussion

Teacher reading of a famous quote or a page or two from a novel featuring a theme or message that parallels the content of the day's lesson

Consequences

Warning

Stern eye contact

Hand gestures

Hall conference

Phone call to a parent and a parent conference

Incentives

High fives

Opportunities such as "Letters to the Editor"

Coronation into the Writers' Guild

Sodas and Walkmans placed into the regular routine of the day

Cues

Hand raised

Eye contact

Saying, "Ladies and Gentlemen."

Waving my hand a certain way means "I'll get to you later," "Move over there," and "Stop [a particular activity]."

Touch a shoulder or desk so student ends the action deemed inappropriate.

INSTRUCTION

Lessons

Instructional strategies

Mix lecture with discussion, debate, research, writing, and role-playing.

Plan active student involvement in lessons with questions, board work, hands-on activities, and group work.

Foster participation through comments, concerns, opinions, and criticisms.

Provide demonstrations.

Provide purpose for learning material.

Dare to be different.

Plan materials to interest students.

Individualized instructional strategies

Offer multiple assignments.

Offer multiple ways of completing assignments.

I have always treated all my students—"at risk," "average," and "gifted"—as individuals. Each student possesses special talents that can compensate for weaknesses. For example, I offer oral tests if a student does not do well on written exams. If a student cannot write a letter to the editor, he or she can draw a political cartoon or give an oral presentation. The course is tailored to meet students' needs.

Questioning strategies

First ask who, what, where, and when. Then ask why, how, and what are your perceptions.

Play devil's advocate.

Examples of questions

If the U.S. history topic is Manifest Destiny, I ask someone to define it, when and where did it occur, and who was involved. Then I ask what was the intent of Manifest Destiny, why was it so eagerly embraced, and was it cruel? What was accomplished? How were people helped? How were lives and cultures ruined? Next, I ask, if you were a white pioneer during the period, would you have done differently or would you, too, have become a participant? How can one judge the past fairly? Does America owe anyone an apology? Are we different today?

Responses to students

When a student gives a correct answer

"Right on!"

"Hey, you're so smart, you should be the teacher!"

"I told you that you could do it!"

"You're the greatest!"

"Yea!"

When a student gives a partially correct answer

I approach the desk of the student, get down on my knees, and say, "Add a little more."

"Go on!"

Ask the class to help us out.

When a student gives an incorrect answer

"Keep on trying!"

Provide a hint.

Solicit help from the class.

Student self-evaluation opportunities

Graph grades.

Comment on progress.

Effective Teaching Practices

Building positive relationships

   Between teacher and students

Let students know I want to be here teaching.

Accept/promote student opinions and uniqueness.

Listen to their concerns.

Get to know them.

Be there for them.

Be honest.

Among classmates

Require students to listen to each other.

Accept opinions.

Be sensitive to cultural and individual differences.

Be polite.

"Catch" them being kind to each other.

With parents

Be honest.

Be firm.

Be compassionate.

Show interest in their child.

Strategies to develop student social skills

Model desired behavior.

Don't preach, but simply offer a reason to behave differently.

Strategies to develop student problem-solving and decision-making skills

Get student input.

Allow students to make choices and decisions.

Ask the student what he or she could/should have done.

Strategies to develop student self-control

It begins with the speech, "You will not always have a teacher, preacher, or parent standing before you; consequently, you must learn to accept accountability and develop a healthy sense of self-discipline."

Share examples of self-discipline.

Celebrate student examples of self-discipline.

Preventive discipline strategies

Emphasize the positive.

Be respectful.

Set high expectations.

Be enthusiastic.

Be knowledgeable in the subject matter.

Handle problems immediately.

Classroom technology plan

> *Use the Internet for research.*
>
> *Use e-mail for correspondence.*
>
> *Use the VCR for tapes.*

ASSESSMENT

Grading plan

> *I strive to have four recorded grades per week. A minimum of two are quizzes. Tests, papers, projects, and oral presentations represent the rest.*

Recording grades in the grade book

> *All assignments are graded in green ink, never red.*
>
> *Color-code the grade book: green ink = test; black ink = quiz; purple ink = project*

Homework policy

> *I give homework assignments to prepare students better for a quiz or test. A low grade usually reflects a student's failure to complete the assignment. Some essay questions are initiated or completed at home; failure to submit an essay can leave a negative impression on one's overall average. I am opposed to teacher policies that use homework as a major element in averaging grades.*

Progress reports

> *Students receive progress reports during each grading period.*

Student opportunities to impact grades

> Extra credit: *Yes*
>
> Rewrites: *Yes*
>
> Drop a grade: *Maybe*
>
> Special assignments: *Yes*
>
> Collection of points to be factored into the final grade: *Maybe*

REFLECTION

I spend time reflecting on the highs and lows of the day and formulate strategies to eliminate the lows and maintain the highs. This time usually takes place as I drive from school to my second job. A couple times a year, the faculty/staff participate in inservice training.

Bibliography

Alschuler, A.S. 1980. *School discipline: A socially literate solution*. New York: McGraw-Hill.

Bloom, B. 1956. *Taxonomy of educational objectives. Handbook I: Cognitive domain*. New York: David McKay, Co., Inc.

Bosch, K.A. 1991. Cooperative learning: Instructions and procedures to assist middle school teachers. *Middle School Journal*, 22 (3):34–35.

Bosch, K.A. and K. Kersey. 1993. Teaching problem-solving strategies. *Clearing House*, 66 (4):228–230.

Bosch, K.A. and K. Kersey. 1994. *The first year teacher: Teaching with confidence*. Washington, D.C.: NEA Professional Library, National Education Association.

Bowers, C.A. and D.J. Flinders. 1990. *Responsive teaching: An ecological approach to classroom patterns of language, culture, and thought*. New York: Teachers College Press.

Boyer, E.L. 1995. *The basic school*. Princeton, New Jersey: The Carnegie Foundation for the Advancement of Teaching.

Brigham, F., A.K. Renfro, and M.M. Brigham. 1994. *Instruction and classroom management: A combination that is music to your ears*. ERIC Document Reproduction Service No. ED 374 109.

Brophy, J. 1981. Teacher praise: A functional analysis. *Review of Educational Research*, 51:5–32.

Burke, K. 1992. *What to do with the kid who . . . .* Arlington Heights, Illinois: IRI/SkyLight Training and Publishing, Inc.

Canter, L. and M. Canter. 1976. *Assertive discipline*. Santa Monica, California: Lee Canter & Associates.

Charles, C.M. 1999. *Building classroom discipline*. 6th ed. New York: Longman.

Cruickshank, D. 1987. *Reflective teaching: The preparation of students of teaching*. Reston, Virginia: Association of Teacher Educators.

Edwards, C.H. 1997. *Classroom discipline and management*. Upper Saddle River, New Jersey: Prentice Hall.

Elam, S., L.C. Rose, and A. M. Gallup. 1997. the 28th annual Phi Delta Kappa/Gallop Poll of the public's attitudes toward the public schools. In Education 97/98: The annual editions series, edited by F. Schultz, pp. 26–43. Guilford, Connecticut: Dushkin Publishing Group, Inc./McGraw-Hill.

Evertson, C. M. 1989. Improving elementary classroom management: A school-based training program for beginning the year. *Journal of Educational Research*, 83:82–90.

Evertson, C. M. 1995. *Classroom organization and management program.* (Revalidation Submission to the Program Effectiveness panel). Washington, D.C.: U.S. Department of Education. (ERIC Document Reproduction Service No. ED 403 247)

Evertson, C.M., E.T. Emmer, B.S. Clements et al. 1989. *Classroom management for elementary teachers.* Englewood Cliffs, New Jersey: Prentice Hall.

Emmer, E.T., C.M. Evertson, J.P. Sanford et al. 1989. *Classroom management for secondary teachers.* Englewood Cliffs, New Jersey: Prentice Hall.

Gardner, H. 1993. *Multiple intelligences: The theory in practice.* New York: BasicBooks.

Glasser, W. 1969. *Schools without failure.* New York: Harper & Row.

Glasser, W. 1986. *Control theory in the classroom.* New York: Harper & Row.

Glasser, W. 1993. *The quality school teacher.* New York: Harper Perennial.

Jones, V.F. and L.S. Jones. 1995. *Comprehensive classroom management.* Needham Heights, Massachusetts: Allyn and Bacon.

Kohn, A. 1996. *Beyond discipline: From compliance to community.* Alexandria, Virginia: Association of Supervision and Curriculum Development.

Kounin, J. 1977. *Discipline and group management in classrooms.* (Rev. ed.). New York: Holt, Rinehart & Winston.

Morehead, M. and D. Cropp. 1994. Enhancing preservice observation experience with structured clinical experiences. *The Teacher Educator,* 29(4):2–8.

Reed, A.J.S. and V.E. Bergemann. 1995. *In the classroom.* (2nd ed.). Guilford, Connecticut: Dushkin Publishing Group, Inc.

Rose, L.C. and A.M. Gallup. 1998. The 30th annual Phi Delta Kappa/ Gallup Poll of the public's attitudes toward the public schools. *Phi Delta Kappan,* 80(1):41–56.

Rowe, M. 1974. Wait-time and rewards as instructional variables: Their influence on language, logic, and fate control. Part one, wait-time. *Journal of Research in Science Teaching,* 11:81–94.

Schon, D. 1983. *The reflective practitioner: How professionals think in action.* New York: BasicBooks.

Sylwester, R.A. 1995. *Celebration of neurons.* Alexandria, Virginia: Association of Supervision and Curriculum Development.

Tobin, K. 1987. The role of wait time in higher cognitive level learning. *Review of Education Research,* 57:69–95.

Veenman, S. 1984. Perceived problems of beginning teachers. *Review of Education Research,* 54:143–178.

Wang, M.C., G.D. Haertel and H.J. Walberg. 1994. What helps students learn? *Educational Leadership,* 51(4):74–79.

Wong, H. and R. Wong. 1998. *The first days of school.* Mountain View, California: Harry Wong Publications, Inc.

Wong, L. 1990. Trainees' perceptions of competence and control in teaching. Paper presented to the International Council on Education for Teaching. July 27–31, 1990. Singapore, China.

Index

There are
one-story intellects,
two-story intellects, and
three-story intellects with skylights.

All fact collectors, who have no aim beyond their
facts, are

one-story minds.

Two-story minds
compare, reason, generalize,
using the labors of the fact collectors
as well as their own.

Three-story minds
idealize, imagine, predict—their best illumination
comes from above,

through the **skylight**.

—Oliver Wendell Holmes

SkyLight
Professional
Development